# Prose & Poetry
## *of*
# SHYLOCK

# Prose & Poetry
## *of*
# SHYLOCK

SHYLOCK

# PROSE & POETRY OF SHYLOCK

iUniverse books may be ordered through booksellers or by contacting:

iUniverse
1663 Liberty Drive
Bloomington, IN 47403
www.iuniverse.com
1-800-Authors (1-800-288-4677)

ISBN: 978-1-5320-3961-4 (sc)
ISBN: 978-1-5320-3960-7 (e)

Library of Congress Control Number: 2017919070

Print information available on the last page.

iUniverse rev. date: 01/26/2018

# Contents

## AUNTIE SAYS

Preface ................................................................................. xvii

## PROSE OF THE TIMES

A Flag Going To Tatters, High Time! (In Prose) ........................... 1
A Loose Cannon (In Prose) ........................................................ 2
A Man's Word (In Prose) .......................................................... 3
A Never-Ending Struggle (In Prose) .......................................... 4
About Good And Evil, A Prayer (In Prose ................................. 5
Africa, The Black Empress (In Prose) ........................................ 6
Allegory Of A Crusade In Merica (In Prose) ............................... 7
Allegory Of - From A King To A Tree And
A Fact-Checker As An Ax (In Prose) .......................................... 8
Of Putin, The Man Upstairs, Power-Drunk And
Is Crimea The Night He Falls Asleep? (In Prose) ...................... 10
Allegory Of The Mad Crusader (In Prose) ............................... 11
Allegory Of The Overvalued Stock (In Prose) .......................... 12
Amputated Justice For Oscar Pistorius (In Prose) .................... 13
An Allegory Of A Shinning City On A Hill (In Prose) .............. 14
An Error Of American Conservatism (In Prose) ........................ 15
And We Are Left Wondering Why (In Prose) ............................ 16
As The Aura Of Celebrity Fades With Age (In Prose) ................ 17
Assad, Exposed As Keeper Of The Corridor Of
Hate In Syria And Survival Of That Crocodile (In Prose) .......... 18
At Last, Hoodie Again (In Prose) ............................................. 19
Baltimore, Another Lighthouse (In Prose) ............................... 20
Beauty Pays (In Prose) ............................................................ 21
Blame Tyrants For The Terrorists, Not Us (In Prose) ............... 22
Chivalry, The Gist (In Prose) .................................................. 23
Commemorating What (In Prose) ........................................... 24

Control Your Destiny (In Prose) .................................................. 25

Curbing Your Enthusiasm (In Prose) ......................................... 26

Deserving The Leader They Chose,
The Curse Of The Ill-Gotten (In Prose) ..................................... 27

Destitute, For Not Being A Man (In Prose) ............................... 28

Diffusion Of Responsibility (In Prose) ...................................... 29

Doubting Thomas And The Arab Spring (In Prose) ................... 30

Even The Devil Cited The Scripture For His Own
Evil Purpose In Biblical Time (In Prose) .................................... 31

God, Help Us! (In Prose) ........................................................... 32

Good Try And Goodbye Assad (In Prose) .................................. 33

Government By Gunmen Has Always Failed (In Prose) ............. 34

Her Consuming Passion (In Prose) ............................................ 35

Her Virgin Voyage (In Prose) .................................................... 36

Homosexuality (In Prose) .......................................................... 37

Honor Or To Honor (In Prose) .................................................. 38

How Did This Happen? (In Prose) ............................................. 39

How Times Have Changed! (In Prose) ....................................... 40

Invisible Shackles (In Prose) ...................................................... 41

King Of The Beasts (In Prose) ................................................... 42

Lesser Than A Beast (In Prose) .................................................. 43

Let The Music Play (In Prose) ................................................... 44

Let Us Not Fool Ourselves (In Prose) ....................................... 45

Loyalty (In Prose) ...................................................................... 46

Lustful Dreams (In Prose) ......................................................... 47

Moments (In Prose) ................................................................... 48

Mopes Of A Jilted Lover (In Prose) ........................................... 49

Muslim People Are Like Rag Dolls (In Prose) ........................... 50

Nothing Is Impossible (In Prose) .............................................. 51

Notoriety, Another Face Of Evil (In Prose) ............................... 52

Old Age (In Prose) ..................................................................... 53

Once More (In Prose) ................................................................ 54

Persuasion (In Prose) ................................................................. 55

Politics With The Poetic Oratory (In Prose) .............................. 56

Principles Over Politics, Anytime! (In Prose) ............................ 58

Putin, Hero To Many, Even In The Usa (In Prose) .................... 59

Racial Profiling, That Insidious, Evil Thing (In Prose)..............60
Right & Wrong, Good & Bad (In Prose).....................................61
Senility, Betrayer Of The Unconscious (In Prose) ....................63
Sheepdogs (In Prose)................................................................64
That Bad Liberal Thing (In Prose) ...........................................65
That Is Who He Is (In Prose).....................................................66
That Perverse Voice (In Prose)..................................................67
The American (Anti-Feminist) Patriarchy (In Prose)................68
The Beast Within (In Prose)......................................................69
The Candidate (In Prose) ..........................................................70
The Cynic (In Prose) .................................................................71
The Elusive, Kissing Flower (In Prose) .....................................72
The Head Of The Spear (In Prose) ...........................................73
The Innocent Child (In Prose) .................................................75
The Iraq War, A Short Story (In Prose) ....................................76
The Kkk Lives! (In Prose)..........................................................78
The Last Gasp Of A Patriarchy! (In Prose) ...............................79
The Lone Kayaker (In Prose).....................................................81
The Man Cave (In Prose) ..........................................................82
The New Terror Army, Isis,
Winning The War On Terror? (In Prose) ..................................83
The Outsider (In Prose).............................................................85
The Reincarnation Of Evil And Assad (In Prose)......................86
The Rise, Then Fall, As The Crusader (In Prose)........................87
The Scourge Of Tyranny (In Prose) ..........................................88
The Status Quo And The Police (In Prose)................................89
The Time He Discovered He Had
A Crazy Haitian Wife (In Prose)................................................90
The Wool Been Cast Off (In Prose) ..........................................93
Things (In Prose) ......................................................................94
This Fbi Philosophy (In Prose)..................................................95
Those Wise Men (In Prose) .......................................................96
True Love (In Prose) ..................................................................97
Tyranny (In Prose) ....................................................................98
Vice (In Prose) ..........................................................................99
What Do They Expect, She Is The Teflon Lady! (In Prose).......100

When Anticipation Was Happiness (In Prose) ........................... 101
When Doubtfulness Becomes Stubbornness
That Can Kill (In Prose) ......................................................... 102
When Love Was A Prison (N Prose) ....................................... 103
Why We Are Here (In Prose) ................................................... 104
Wonders, Truly Never Cease (In Prose) .................................. 105
Your Memory (In Prose) ......................................................... 107

## POEMS

A Beckoning Hand .................................................................. 111
A Call To Poets ....................................................................... 112
A Fleeting Beauty ................................................................... 113
A Jealous Moon ...................................................................... 114
A Lasting Flame ...................................................................... 115
A Little Boy & Three Angels ................................................... 116
A Shaken Faith O Lord ........................................................... 117
A Tale Of Terror ..................................................................... 118
A Tragedy We Grieve .............................................................. 119
A Wonderful, Glorious Reverie .............................................. 120
After The Storm ...................................................................... 121
After This Winter .................................................................... 122
All Tyranny By The Weak ....................................................... 123
Allegory Of Town Of Kobani ................................................. 124
Ambiguous Ambivalence ........................................................ 125
America's Nightmare ............................................................... 126
An Allegory Of Redemption ................................................... 127
Another Day But The Same ..................................................... 128
Autumn ................................................................................... 129
Autumn Looms ....................................................................... 130
Ballad Of A Sex Addict ........................................................... 131
Ballad Of Bean Counters ........................................................ 132
Ballad Of Go Bomb The Evil Bandits ..................................... 133
Ballad Of New Cow Was Old Cow .......................................... 135
Ballad Of That Celtic Thing ................................................... 136
Ballad Of The Emanuel Nine .................................................. 137

Ballad Of The Gambler.................................................. 138
Ballad Of The Hitman.................................................. 139
Ballad Of The Pontiff.................................................. 140
Ballad Of The Stuntman............................................. 141
Ballad Of The Surfer.................................................. 142
Ballad Of The Tantra Dance..................................... 143
Ballad Of Two Wretched Souls................................. 144
Ballad Of What Is To Be ........................................... 145
Bart, Tess And The Wind .......................................... 146
Battles Of Civil Disobedience................................... 147
Beautiful Hummingbird............................................. 148
Bittersweet Mother Nature ....................................... 149
Brain-Snatcher ........................................................... 150
Chant For Change ......................................................151
Chivalry Still Alive! ................................................... 152
Dementia, Ye Old Demon .......................................... 153
Desire .......................................................................... 154
Earth To Man.............................................................. 155
Enterprise.................................................................... 156
Essence Of Life ........................................................... 157
Evil And The Uneasy Head......................................... 158
Flame-Arrows ............................................................. 159
For That Same Love .................................................. 160
For What Good Then Is Life!...................................... 161
Forever, Slaves............................................................. 162
Freddie Gray, A Martyr Made .................................... 163
Gargoyles.....................................................................164
Good, Old Nostalgia .................................................. 165
Goodbye Winter Welcome Spring .............................. 166
Grandson..................................................................... 167
Hammer Away............................................................. 168
Heartbreaking Voodoo Girl........................................ 169
His Wife And Christmas ............................................ 170
How They Want.......................................................... 171
Hubris.......................................................................... 172
Inevitability ................................................................ 173

Iowans, Help Us!..................................................... 174

It ............................................................................ 175

It's Dancehall ....................................................... 176

Jamaican Nostalgia ............................................... 177

Joy........................................................................... 178

Karl And Kim ........................................................ 179

Kinesthesia............................................................ 180

Levity..................................................................... 181

Life's Fleeting Ways .............................................. 182

Life's Twists & Turns ............................................ 183

Litle Birdie ............................................................ 184

Love ....................................................................... 185

Mandela And The Power Of One ............................. 186

Miss Me ................................................................. 187

More Of Winter's Ironies...................................... 188

Mortified .............................................................. 189

My Lovely ............................................................. 190

My Muse................................................................ 191

My Smile Maker ................................................... 192

Nature's Trick ....................................................... 193

Novelty .................................................................. 194

Nymph And The Beast ........................................... 195

O Gentle Knights Of Yore ..................................... 196

O Fate!................................................................... 197

O What A Charade!............................................... 198

O, Sweet Bel Canto............................................... 199

Oblivion ................................................................200

Ode To A Prayer Warrior....................................... 201

Ode To A Sinner................................................... 202

Ode To A Warrior's Wife ...................................... 203

Ode To America! ...................................................204

Ode To Chivalry....................................................205

Ode To The Backstabbers ......................................206

Oh, How I Miss.....................................................207

Old Dog, New Trick..............................................208

Old Glory (Usa).....................................................209

On Death Row ................................................ 210
On The Catwalk .............................................. 211
On Tyrants (Castro Etc) .................................... 212
Out Of The Mouths Of Babes ............................. 213
Police Brutality .............................................. 214
Pretty Girls .................................................. 215
Requiem For A Despot ...................................... 216
Revolution ................................................... 217
Say Goodbye To Thunderstorms ......................... 218
Sex .......................................................... 219
She, His Nemesis ............................................220
Shingles ..................................................... 221
Shredded Some Old Memories ............................222
Slaves Of Tyranny...........................................223
So Much More To Devour...................................224
Sonnet Of A Stronger Love.................................225
Sonnet Of Another Day.....................................226
Sonnet Of Beauty And The Wild...........................227
Sonnet Of Cold Swashbuckler .............................228
Sonnet Of Come Away With Me............................229
Sonnet Of Heartbreak, That Silent Killer .................230
Sonnet Of Hoodie, Thy Son ............................... 231
Sonnet Of O, Dark Day At The Tower .................... 232
Sonnet Of Only Time Will Tell.............................233
Sonnet Of Santana...........................................234
Sonnet Of Spirit Of Old Glory.............................235
Sonnet Of The Black Stallion...............................236
Sonnet Of The Bluebirds....................................237
Sonnet Of The Daring, Damned Devil .....................238
Sonnet Of The Decider......................................239
Sonnet Of The Elements....................................240
Sonnet Of The Great Beyond...............................241
Sonnet Of The Now..........................................242
Sonnet Of The Renaissance .................................243
Sonnet Of The Scary Night Of A 7-Year-Old..............244
Sonnet Of The Tempest & The Crew.......................245

Sonnet Of The "Tinsel Hair" Ogre .................................................246
Sonnet Of This Is Hell .................................................................247
Steatopygia .................................................................................248
Stimming On Life ........................................................................249
Tears Of Joy .................................................................................250
That Forever Thing ......................................................................251
That Ole Chivalry, The Reunion ..................................................252
That Passion ................................................................................253
That Taste Of Strawberries ..........................................................254
The Battle Of Ptsd .......................................................................255
The Bear And The Eagle ...............................................................256
The Beggars .................................................................................257
The Bogeywoman .........................................................................258
The Brinkmen ..............................................................................259
The Cycle Of Life .........................................................................260
The Dauntless ..............................................................................261
The Dive Of The Countdown .......................................................262
The Erotic Love ...........................................................................263
The Falling Tear Drop ..................................................................264
The Feminist ................................................................................265
The Glorified Drag Queen ............................................................266
The Great Escape .........................................................................267
The Greatest Still .........................................................................268
The Heterosexual Boy ..................................................................269
The Joy Of Words ........................................................................270
The Little Sun Catcher .................................................................271
The Lone Wolves ..........................................................................272
The Milky Way .............................................................................273
The Old Lady & The Grim Reaper ...............................................274
The Old Lady Upstairs .................................................................275
The Old Man ...............................................................................276
The Pauper & The Poet ................................................................277
The Preacher ................................................................................278
The Rebels ...................................................................................279
The Rise Of The Teflon Lady ........................................................280
The Sorceress ...............................................................................281

The Sun Vs. The Wind ................................................................ 282

The Survivor ............................................................................ 283

The Teflon Lady & The "Tinsel Hair" Ogre ........................... 284

The Thug .................................................................................. 285

The Way You Smile ................................................................... 286

Their Triad Tryst ...................................................................... 287

Then Over In Damascus ........................................................... 288

Then Over In Moscow .............................................................. 289

There're Souls In Limbo .......................................................... 290

Things We Built ....................................................................... 291

This Apple Madness .................................................................. 292

This Cycle Of Hate ................................................................... 293

This Temple .............................................................................. 294

Those Feet ................................................................................ 295

Those Glory Days ..................................................................... 296

Those God-Players ................................................................... 297

Those Hands I Trust ................................................................ 298

Those Lifelines ......................................................................... 299

Those Sacred Oaths .................................................................. 300

Those Tiny Tots ....................................................................... 301

Those Trumpeters .................................................................... 302

Time Of Halloween .................................................................. 303

Tingle With Love ...................................................................... 304

'Tis Nature's Fault ................................................................... 305

To The Arabs Fighting For Freedom ........................................ 306

Toddler .................................................................................... 307

Tragedy Of The Hearts ............................................................ 308

Twice The Man ........................................................................ 309

Two Knights And Ol' Chivalry ................................................ 310

Typoland .................................................................................. 311

Unrequited Love, No Longer (Bart To Tess) ........................... 312

Until She Met Old Nick ........................................................... 313

Until You Met Her Shrew ........................................................ 314

Warning! .................................................................................. 315

Watch Us Banter ...................................................................... 316

Waves ....................................................................................... 317

We See You ............................................................. 318

Wedded ................................................................. 319

What A Fool ........................................................... 320

What Better Way To Die ......................................... 321

What Did She See In Me? ......................................... 322

What Manner Of Men ............................................. 323

What Would Have Been, If He Had? ......................... 324

When Demons Zoom ............................................... 325

When Evil Was Enemy ............................................. 326

When Love Came Knocking ...................................... 327

When Passion Cries ................................................. 328

Whither, Blind Lady ............................................... 329

Windows Of Life ..................................................... 330

Winter'S Tail .......................................................... 331

Women .................................................................. 332

Your Lives Matter Too ............................................. 333

# AUNTIE SAYS

# PREFACE

Auntie Says, "God has got to be a woman". Jokingly, of course, she says she arrived at this conclusion as she observes Acts of God or Mother Nature, a nurturing Mother Nature and Human Nature which comes from her. How the scripture says "God is a jealous God" etc. And so Auntie exclaims, "God is a woman", as in blaming a bitchy Mother Nature, whenever her plans are upset for whatever reasons.

So who is Auntie? Auntie is my big sister, Hopus. My children, Maria, Bud and their younger sister, Marie, who are now adults, discovered in their teens (roughly 9 years apart) that their Auntie Hopie was witty and very cynical. And over the years, they would repeat to me what she would say to them off the cuff, about life, things, humans and other creatures etc. and her pithy remarks would always enlighten them. I had known all my life that my sister was very smart but it wasn't until my children's discovery that my curiosity was piqued about her utterances and so I started paying more attention. I have included some of her witticisms and cynicisms in this book to share with readers as prose and I hope you will find them as enlightening and enjoyable as my children and I do....... Shylock

ON CRIME – Auntie says, "The Police with intelligence don't use the intelligence themselves. What they do, they give the intelligence to unintelligent officers to interpret it and so we, the public suffer."

ON TERRORISM – Auntie says, "One man's terrorist, is another man's freedom-fighter."

ON DISTRESS – Auntie says, "Just say to yourself that, this too will pass, whenever you find yourself in any distressful situation."

ON OUR UNCLE CHARLES – "It will really be ashes to ashes and dust to dust, when we bury his ashes." Uncle Charles was cremated in the USA and his ashes taken in an urn to Jamaica, W.I. to be buried.

ON THE ANTS AND THE COCKROACH – Auntie says, "Leave them alone, they don't need your help," when I told her that the ants were struggling to take a dead cockroach through a crack in a wall as food. "They have been doing it for thousands of years," she said.

ON THE WEST INDIES CRICKET TEAM – Auntie says, "The players think cricket is a game." She said this because the team had been losing most of its matches for the season. "It's a war," she said.

ON ALL THINGS IN LIFE THAT WERE ONCE NEW – Auntie says, "Every new T-Shirt becomes a duster-cloth," An analogy she uses to explain that nothing and no one are indispensible or last forever.

ON MY FRIEND WHO WAS HAVING A PROBLEM WITH HIS GIRLFRIEND AND TOLD ME ABOUT IT – Auntie says, "Next thing, a monkey jumps on your shoulder," when I told her I am staying outside the forest so I can see the trees, meaning, I will not get involved with my friend's problem. I will only listen and give advice to the best of my ability.

ON THE PERSON HANDLING COMPLAINTS FOR EMPLOYEES AT A LABOR-INTENSIVE COMPANY – Auntie says, "That person is really a pest-controller," when I was explaining the importance of that person's job in solving employees' problems.

ON OUR REBELLIOUS COUSIN – Auntie says, "Some people "love" people who don't like them," when I asked her how come everybody, for example, his father, aunt Evelyn and others love him so much.

ON SECRETS ABOUT YOUR FRIENDS – Auntie says, "Never tell back your friends, the things they tell you in secret about themselves, they would never trust you again."

ON THE WASHING MACHINE – Auntie says, "Mama turned us into 4-hand people when she installed a washing machine in the house. Now we can cook and wash at the same time and better yet, we can sleep and wash at the same time."

ON THE SAYING THAT TWO HEADS ARE BETTER THAN ONE – Auntie says, "Not true, one head is better than two because you need to put your heads together as one to cooperate to get things done."

ON LEGS – Auntie says, "The most important legs in the world are the legs of a racehorse and a ballerina."

ON HER BOSS – Auntie says, "It is typical of him to send a memo without thought," when the office received an email from Miami where he is staying, advising the office that he sent them a separate email with a memo attached with a thought for the week but when the email with a memo arrived, no thought could be found.

ON TRIPLETS – Auntie says, "That is because two is a team and three is a crowd," when I asked her how come we never heard of any famous triplets.

ON HURRICANE KATRINA – Auntie says, "Katrina took everyone by storm."

ON MISTAKES – Auntie says, "Those who don't make mistakes are doing nothing."

ON VACATION LEAVE FROM YOUR JOB – Auntie says, "Those who can stay away from a job for three weeks should be concerned that the job doesn't need them."

ON HARD DRUGS – Auntie says, "Those who use them can't not do without them and cannot do without them."

ON BREAST-FEEDING – Auntie says, "Mothers should breast-feed their children because cow's milk is for cows and the milk from your mother's breast is for humans."

ON WIDOWERS – Auntie Says, "Never marry a widower because it is likely that he contributed to his situation."

ON OUR OLD DOG JOHNNY – Auntie says, "Listen to you, just like a man," when I told her to spay the female dog instead of neutering Johnny, after she told me of her plans to neuter him to protect him from injuries during heat periods of the female dog. And Auntie says, "you would even change an established practice to protect Johnny," when I told her that it was beauty before age, in referring to female dog and Johnny. Then Auntie says, "I know it as age before beauty."

ON BAD GRAMMAR BY AMERICANS, HEARD ON TV TALK SHOWS AND IN THE MOVIES - Auntie says, "The reason some Jamaicans speak better English than most Americans is, the Americans kicked "the English" out about two centuries before the Jamaicans did. The Americans did it in 1776 and the Jamaicans, in 1962."

ON COLORS – Auntie says, "Without light everything is black. Even in the mind's eye you need light and if you don't believe me, ask someone who has never seen."

ON ME REMINDING HER ABOUT WATER BOILING ON THE STOVE - Auntie says, "What can I do with him? I know what I cannot do without him."

ON OUR OLD BROKEN DOWN FRIDGE – Auntie says, "The thing is dead, long live the thing," when I told her "pull the plug" and let us put it to rest.

ON BEING AT HOME ALONE – Auntie says, "Whenever you are overseas (she lives alone and I stay at her place for a while), the night prowlers think I have company when I am working at home on my dictating machine. I hear you can fool some of the people some of the time etc."

ON HER CREATIVITY – Auntie says, "You mean genes," when I said to her that she has our mother's energy, flair and imagination in doing things, that she has her "genius."

ON HER FRIEND WHO IS MORALLY LOOSE – Aunties says, "Shylock, she and I are different. I have been there but I haven't done that," when I suggested to her that she should counsel her friend.

ON THE PHRASE "SEEING IS BELIEVING" – Auntie says, "You won't believe THIS unless you see THAT and you won't believe THAT unless you see THIS." We were watching an item on the show "Believe It Or Not" involving a dog that can sniff out cancerous cells in humans.

ON THE MOVIE "BROKE BACK MOUNTAIN" WHICH IS ABOUT TWO HOMOSEXUAL COWBOYS – Auntie says, "No more John Wayne, Lone Ranger, The Good, The Bad and The Ugly and Hop Along Cassidy, those were real cowboys."

ON THINGS SHE HAD TO DO FOR ME - Auntie says, "There is nothing "now" about this process so please have a little heart when you are giving me orders. Stop trying to "things to do" my life. Remember me, Hopic, who does not wear a watch," when I urged her to do a "Things to Do" list.

ON HER ACADEMIC ACCOMPLISHMENTS AND HOW THAT INSPIRED TWO GENERATIONS OF OURS. – Auntie says, "That is the power of one," when I drew her attention to it.

ABOUT THE WALL STREET BAILOUT 2008 – Auntie says, when she wrote, to me," I see the Republican Party is becoming socialist. Who would have thought that!!!!! Bailout!!!!! Bah! Humbug!"

ON THE MEDIA AND COUNTRY – Auntie says, "You know that I am something of a cynic and pessimist. We have discussed, you and I, the propensity of the media to give away secrets in the name of informing the public about "intelligence" and this is so stupid. The enemy is within! The Jamaican media are following hard on this practice. It is called "competition, press freedom, the edge, the bottom line" reputation. They don't give a damn about country! Remember after 9/11 there was one network which put a reporter in an airport and the cockpit of an aircraft to show the world and the enemy (internal and external) all the new safety features and plans to combat terrorism. I do not know if you remember how that got my goat."

ON COMMON SENSE – Auntie says, "If common sense was really common, everybody would have it."

ON PRESIDENT OBAMA'S POLICY AND SPEECH – "Shylock, see if you can get a hold of President Obama and tell, a great American President once said, "one cannot make the poor rich by making the rich poor". Another thing, please tell him that the indefinite article becomes "an" before a silent "h" (an honest man) and vowels except "u" eu, ew and the word "one" and it can also be used before unstressed syllables (an historian). It's tricky. Remember English is not the American's language. He goes out of his way to say things like (a opening) (a ever-growing). It annoys me so. He is an orator, he should know the basics. Listen to him for five minutes and you are bound to hear these errors. His voice is wonderful so the captivated will not hear the errors. I really admire him but the "an" thing annoys me."

ON THE SAYING, TO KILL TWO BIRDS WITH ONE STONE – Auntie says, "I prefer to use one stone to kill two birds. Is that not violent in its imagery? It sounds impossible too. I bet you don't realize the ridiculous truism of that imagery (killing two birds with one stone} and how improbable it looks, making one appear cruel and inept. All about the imagery, I will never use the saying again."

ON PRESIDENT OBAMA APPOINTING SONIA SOTOMAYOR AS ASSOCIATE JUSTICE TO THE US SUPREME COURT – Auntie says, in a message to Republicans. "The selection for Supreme Court Judge is a smart move. Go with it! It is history making! Be careful how you quarrel with it or you will stay in the wilderness for years. Hispanics, like blacks, use sex for recreation. They have an abundance of children = voters. America will soon have only brown people. The Republicans had better wake up."

ON MY SECOND BOOK, POEMS OF SHYLOCK AND ON THE WRITING OF MY THIRD, PROSE & POETRY OF SHYLOCK– Auntie says, "I bet that you have not been marketing. Did you sell any copies of your book? Remember to keep the poems either universal or epic. If they are too family-oriented your market will be small. I see that you are now concentrating on words. The refuge of those who have given up trying to do the (9:00 to 5:00), wish to change the world with words (watch Obama) and want to leave a footprint or are getting mad, possibly, one, two, three or all of the above. I know that you are laughing your head off. You cannot believe my insights!"

ON MICHAEL JACKSON AFTER HIS DEATH – Auntie Says, "I am still in two minds about him, this man-boy. His death marks the end of the era of Superstars. I believe he will remain a "Thriller" for the years to come."

ON THE EXPRESSION "PRAY TELL" – Auntie says, when I asked her what it meant, "Shylock, it simply means, "Please tell me". It is a sarcastic way of asking a question especially, when one does not want to hear the answer and when the answer is expected to be nonsense, illogical, presumptuous or an irritant. One simply throws one's head back looks down one's nose, close one's eyes briefly, looks askance, assumes a stance of authority, stiffens one's neck and/or one's body, utters the words "pray tell" in a slow, proper, cultured and scornful tone, awaits the nonsense, rubbish, or irritant anticipated and assumes an air of utter contempt. It's a girls' thing. Ask Marie (my daughter, 20-year-old at the time) what it means, "unaware that my daughter had just given me a lesson in "Pray Tell" and it was pretty much how Auntie described it, to boot!.

ON HER JOB – Auntie says, "Remember despite everything, I still work on a plantation and have to work to a "kill dead" time. Ask the slaves who missed a step on the treadmill. They are all in heaven. Ask anyone of them. My job is also like an abusive husband. It is very jealous and does not allow me time to dawdle. It is a time-service factory job with ever-complaining clients (local and overseas) rushing us all day demanding perfect credit reports in the shortest time. It is a thankless job. I am going to die doing a thankless, low-paying rump of a job. My choice! Like in the case of most abused wives, the abusive husband brings home the cash. We could take this analogy to great lengths. It is an apt one."

ON TEACHING ME TO PRONOUNCE THE FRENCH PHRASE "A BIENTOT" – Aunties says, "Pronounce "A" like "a" in apple. Bientot is a combination of the verb to "Be" joined to a shortened "on" and your big "toe' = A Be on toe. Do you like my phonetics? Try it on Evelyne (she is referring to my Haitian French-speaking wife). Remember the French do not pronounce the single "t" at the end of a word. That is why it is "toe" and not a tiny "tot"

ON WRTING ME A HAND-WRITTEN LETTER AND ENCLOSING A FORM TO BE FILLED OUT

MANUALLY – Auntie says, "Really interesting! If the next generation or two get hold of this letter, they would wonder why I had to pen a letter. Penning a letter! What is that? Better yet, the next generation or two will also wonder why I had to send a Form. Old history, our present day."

ON SENDING ME THIS EMAIL FROM HER OFFICE ABOUT MY JAMAICAN DRIVER'S LICENCE SHE IS LOOKING ABOUT FOR ME AND I HAD TO SENT HER A PICTURE ETC.– Auntie says, "As long as you do not look like a convict it's all right. My advice is that you take another decent photograph. You might not be able to quickly convince the Police that you are you. MOREOVER MY MESSENGER WILL BE HELPING ME. I DO NOT WANT HER TO BELIEVE THAT MY BROTHER LOOKS LIKE AN OLD LADY. I AM NOT SHOUTING THE DAMN CAPS KEY HAS STUCK. IT GIVES TROUBLE SOMETIMES. I find that some keyboards are not ready. Some trouble with this one at the office. Continuing......On the other hand, the camera though unkind, does not lie."

ON GETTING OLD – Auntie says, "As one gets older all one can say is "That's life" and fall back on "Everything is for a good".

ON MY ASKING HER WHAT WAS MEANT BY "BEATING AROUND THE BUSH" INSTEAD OF "BEATING ABOUT THE BUSH", IN ERROR – Auntie says. "Maybe that was what the new Obama Administration was doing for an excuse… "beating Bush". My interpretation is probably antiquated. I know it as "beating about the bush" i.e. taking things slowly, timid, hesitant, especially about expressing an opinion. Another "beating" which suggest evasiveness is "beating about" or trying to find an excuse. Now "beating around the bush" is a new one. The language evolves. This one sounds like straight trying to avoid, evade, to waste time, to say it diplomatically, to use tact, to prevent an upheaval, to deceive and we could go on but we prefer to stop "beating around the bush" and ask you, what do you want to know the meaning of that for? Be like Alice, make it mean whatever you want it to mean. Whenever you hear anyone say "it is becoming curiouser and curiouser" that is from "Alice's Adventures in Wonderland" or "Everything has a moral if you can find it". There are scores of sayings from Alice's Adventures – Lewis Corroll was witty."

ON A USUAL DAY AT HER JOB – Auntie says, "I have not had a second to scratch my head. It is a circular problem, no, not my head, the situation. When one does good work one gets more work to do good. It is literally "doing good" almost like social work (her chosen profession before trying her hand at credit consulting). It seems that I am doom to be a "do gooder".

ON A FAMILY FRIEND WHO COMMITTED SUICIDE – Auntie says, "Rumor has it that he lost millions of dollars in either one or two Ponzi schemes. He could not live with himself. He had been taken for a ride, an expensive, deceitful ride. That kind of loss is hard to take. It is possible that he had invested his family's money and possibly there were other issues. His self-esteem took a beating from the vice, GREED and he probably could not bring himself to cultivate a virtue or strengthen a virtue to counter the vice. That is what the average Joe does but he was not an average Joe. Virtue would probably look like weakness. There is something in the seven virtues and vices. One set elevates the other debases. Please remind your children of these things. What he did may appear selfish but for a man who is not an Islamic Radical, he must be a brave man to decide to call it quits. It would always be a mystery, suicide."

ON BEING OVERWORKED AND KILLING ONESELF – Auntie says, "I suppose people like me commit suicide in acceptable ways. Work until you drop! Don't laugh. Remember the poem, "The Ballad of Reading Gaol", by Oscar Wilde, "For each one kills the thing he loves etc. etc. "some with a bitter look, some with a kiss etc". Same thing with death, each person kills himself in his own way. Some overeat, others drink too much, others sleep too much, others are jealous, some are worried and anxious all the time, some are impatient and you cn add to the list."

ON THE MISHANDLING OF AN EXTRADITION ORDER FROM THE USA FOR JAMAICAN DRUG LORD, CHRISTOPHER COKE aka, DUDUS, BY THEN PRIME MINISTER, BRUCE GOLDING, WHO APPEARED TO BE PROTECTING DUDUS AND WHICH RESULTED IN THE DEATHS OF OVER 100 CITIZENS AND SCORES MAIMED BY THE JAMAICAN SECURUTY FORCES, TO FIND DUDUS WHO WAS STILL AT LARGE – Auntie says, "They put the cart before the horse, Shylock, have you ever heard of anything so upside down? The bottom line is that Bruce Golding is now Humpty Dumpty. The public opprobrium could be cut with a knife! The dolly house pop down! Golding is done! He was probably never a chess player. Could he not see the end of the war? He was on the horns of dilemma. Could he not make the less harmful decision? "Rebel without a cause", I call him. You are looking at "Paradise Lost" (meaning Jamaica). I could never have bent myself to vote for him and his vacillating was the reason. I feel satisfied that my judgment was right."

ON COUNTRY AND CHARACTER – Auntie says, "It's like the character of the country of your origin, is a part of tour own character, that you have to explain and convince others about, especially, when things happen. When they are good, you are like the country and when they are bad, you are different."

ON TRUST AND RESPECT – Auntie says, "Trust and respect I have always said, could be compared to a piece of china pottery (her hobby is pottery), delicate, to be handled with care for once chipped or broken it is done."

ON A CALL TO JURY DUTY AND HER SLAVE-DRIVING BOSS'S ADVICE – Auntie says, "I have a "legal" dilemma. Chungie (nickname for her Chinese boss) would hear nothing of me being away from work for a month at such short notice. You should hear him. Tell them that you cannot hear. Get a doctor to say that you are ill. Tell them this. Tell them that. That effrontery, it all fell on deaf ears. Why? I am going to be a juror for a month."

ON GRAVALICIOUS, A WORD USED TO DESCRIBE SOMEONE WHO IS GREEDY OR AVARICIOUS, IN JAMAICAN DIALECT – Auntie says, "This is really a combination word, isn't sweet? Meaning, grab value and delicious, shortened to gra va licious, combined as gravalicious

ON THE BELIEF THAT WE ARE REWARDED FOR GIVING = Auntie says, "Giving is good and goodness is God!"

# PROSE OF THE TIMES

# A FLAG GOING TO TATTERS, HIGH TIME! (in prose)

From what I have heard about the period in America's history that the Confederate Flag represents, today it is the embodiment of a past that saw the darkest side of America. Unfortunately, many still romanticize about it as humans are wont to do with evil because of revisionism, glorification, short memories, ignorance etc.

We see that with Nazism, the KKK, Terrorism etc. And in the case of the Confederate Flag, we see a "racism" meme as well.

We may shred it but the past lives on, unfortunately!

# A LOOSE CANNON (in prose)

The smallest gun is naked power
and in the wrong hands, it can cause
false courage and a misguided sense
of justice thus rendering the user, A
Loose Cannon among us.

# A MAN'S WORD (in prose)

A man's words and deeds ought to be seen
as working as one, for words can be fleeting
like the winds over the prairies.
His words and his actions should be in lockstep
or at the very least, be like the natural tandem
of lightning and thunder.
Still they ought to be like his own two hands,
clapping in unison, an unmistakable synergy.
Otherwise, avoid such a man.

# A NEVER-ENDING STRUGGLE (in prose)

From the scars of plantations to the scares
of penitentiaries! To you, it's like a game!
But I'll tell you my friend….to them, it's
just the same!
From the pains of segregation to the pangs
of street protests! To you, it's just a shame!
But I'll tell you my friend….to them, it's
like the same!
From civil rights are human rights to the
BLM Movement! To you, it's just a name!.
But I'll tell you my friend….to them, it's
still the same!

# ABOUT GOOD AND EVIL, A PRAYER (in prose

Lord, that good and evil are absolutes
and opposites, then nothing good can
come evil and nothing evil can come
from good, right?
Why then, some of your Believers
say you sometimes unleash evils like
September 11, ISIS, Boko Haram etc.
upon us so as to teach us a lesson
by punishing us?
And that lesson is for us to be good
and come to you.

# AFRICA, THE BLACK EMPRESS (in prose)

With full eyes, full lips, a nose to match, high
cheekbones, this rear chocolate beauty is the
face of Africa.
She embodies the rhythms of a people, among
which are, echoes of the whip, the beating of
the drum, the sounds of the jungle and the beat
of their hearts.
And her voluptuous body, it reflects the natural
beauty of the land, among which are, the curves
and contours of a wonderful landscape, a vibrant
wildlife and the cultural, artistic expressions of
a people.
But she is not perfect for she also personifies
the pain and sufferings of a people too proud
to show it.
Still, she is Africa, The Black Empress.

# ALLEGORY OF A CRUSADE
# IN MERICA (in prose)

Once upon a time, in the year 2016, it was not lost on women and men who were victims of sexual harassment and abuse as children and adults, that an old man who dozens of women said, sexually-harassed and abused them, became the next Supreme Leader of Merica Then suddenly others who were sexually-harassed and abused, now as emboldened female and male accusers, started dragging other accused, these old men, as if by their britches of shame, before the Court of Public Opinion.

But not for financial gain! For you see, the accusers this time are not of the same ilk as those of the past. Many are people of fame and fortune, seeking only, for the accused to be ousted from or relinquish their seats of power. Seats from which they could still be doing to others what was done to them, the accusers.

# ALLEGORY OF - FROM A KING TO A TREE AND A FACT-CHECKER AS AN AX (in prose)

Once there was a King, reigning over a kingdom without borders. His personality was endearing to many and they craved his flamboyance. Even the Fourth Estate (The Press) felt the same way about him and journalists, TV presenters, Talk Radio presenters, reporters etc., would seek his counsel on a range of issues important to life, generally. He usually, inspired confidence in how to get things done and that was most important to some of the people. To them, he was "master of all he surveys."

Those people wanted him for themselves. They wanted him to give up a safe and flourishing kingdom to come and preside over their world of politics and make it safe and flourishing too. So they would ask him. And as a man who relished challenges and saw himself as a world-class negotiator, he did agree to join their world.

Lo and behold, the world of politics proved very difficult for him to rule in. Firstly, he would now hold the Office of a Presidency as a President, which was one third of the separated powers and possibly, a divided government of a Republic. The other two third being, a Congress and a Judiciary. Secondly, he was no longer a King who made all the decisions in his kingdom. He must now conform with laws and generally, consult with the other two third of the government before getting things done. These were time-honored practices and procedures, laid down by the Founders of the Republic, many years ago. Finally, this was all a nightmare for the former King and for a majority of the people too, as it transformed him.

He changed into, The "Tinsel Hair Ogre, figuratively. The experience brought out the worst in him, his true character. Abraham Lincoln, a former President of the Republic, once said, "Nearly all men can stand adversity, but if you want to test a man's character, give him power." I guess in this case, the power was different.

As The "Tinsel Hair" Ogre, some thought he was devoid of "the milk of human kindness." Some thought he lacked empathy, respect for women and other minorities etc. Some thought he was a pathological liar, lying about his own behavior and the behavior of others, including The Press. The same Press that found his personality endearing and craved his flamboyance as King!

Now, to them he was like a Tree! A lying Tree, whose rustle and whispers in the wind, must be fact-checked at all times, by a fact-checker as an ax.

# OF PUTIN, THE MAN UPSTAIRS, POWER-DRUNK AND IS CRIMEA THE NIGHT HE FALLS ASLEEP? (in prose)

Each night the drunkard upstairs would come home at the same time. He would take off one foot of his shoes and drop it on the floor. That would awake the folks sleeping downstairs and they would remain awake until the drunkard takes off the other foot and drop it, then they would go back to sleep. Usually, it would be shortly after the first shoe was dropped.

One night the drunkard dropped the first shoe and the folks woke up and remain awake with bated breath for the other shoe to drop which didn't happen, as the man upstairs fell asleep after taking off the first shoe.

As it turned out, the drunkard would eventually drop the next shoe, Syria.

# ALLEGORY OF THE MAD CRUSADER (in prose)

His mind trapped in a labyrinth of hate, puts
him and his followers in a parallel universe
name, Merica,
Merica, should not be confused with America,
known among other things, as the land of the
free and the promised land and which was
once described by a late, beloved leader as
the shining city on a hill.
Merica, is this place where he as Supreme
Leader and his followers blamed immigrants
and blacks for all its problems and banished
the immigrants, in particular Muslims, back to
whence they came then forbade future entry,
for good. And him, as Supreme Leader?
That could only happen in Merica!

# ALLEGORY OF THE OVERVALUED STOCK (in prose)

And it came to pass, that the Blue Party put forth a nominee, the value of whose stock was known to the public.

For after thirty years of trading up and trading down and withering conspiracy theories were built into her stock, of its real value, the public was apprised.

But the Blue Party did something else.

By party raiding, it would ensure that its opponent, the Red Party, did put forth a nominee, the real value of whose stock was unknown to the public.

Then it proceeded to pick to pieces, the fake value of the Red Party's nominee.

That exposed a lower, true value of his stock, overpriced by the fleeting aura of wealth and celebrity.

# AMPUTATED JUSTICE FOR OSCAR PISTORIUS (in prose)

This double amputee murdered his girlfriend by all accounts including his. According to him, he woke up in the night and didn't see his girlfriend in the bed beside him. Meanwhile, he heard a sound in the bathroom and fired his gun through the bathroom door because he believed it was a burglar in there, when it turned out to be the same girlfriend who wasn't in the bed beside him.

Now, despite his handicap, he is the greatest Olympian in South Africa and it appears there is a very powerful sporting lobby over there that is getting its way thus far to get him out of prison and back on the training field for the next Olympics.
For why then did a Judge without a Jury find him guilty of culpable homicide (manslaughter) when he was charged with murder, which allows him to serve far less time in prison? And how is it he is up for parole before the mandatory one sixth of his sentence served?

Let us see what happens in November 2015 when the Appeal Court hears the Prosecutor's appeal to reverse the findings of the lower Court to murder,
again.

Amputated Justice?

# AN ALLEGORY OF A SHINNING CITY ON A HILL (in prose)

And it came to pass, that the Defenders of The Status Quo, Ole Troglodytes, unleashed the wrath of The Anti-Feminist Patriarchy, personified by The "Tinsel Hair" Ogre, against The Majority and The Teflon Lady, who The Majority favors to lead The Patriarchy.

The ugly, misogynistic beast would grope women, kiss and touch them too, against their will, scare little kids and terrorize ethnic non-while groups with xenophobic threats etc.

And he and the Ole Troglodytes hope to suppress the will of The Majority from choosing The Teflon Lady, with their relentless "witch-hunting" activities against her, along with the help of powerful foreign agencies.

But The Majority doesn't seem to be fazed by their ugly deeds and moral bankruptcy.

It is laser-focused on giving The Teflon Lady a chance to lead, after 240 years of The Anti-Feminist Patriarchy.

# AN ERROR OF AMERICAN CONSERVATISM (in prose)

While the Conservatives rightly defend the character of the of USA as a Republic, they err in their blindness to the role democracy plays in our Republic while repeating our Founding Fathers' utterances in reaction to what occurred in a different epoch, that democracy is the is mob rule.

But not so today and that role is skillfully exploited by Progressives to their advantage.

Democracy is the enduring power of progressivism. Progressives are geniuses in the use of democracy especially the majority rule. They know that the equality of civil rights and fairness are fundamental to democracy and that all free societies eventually evolve in that direction.

Hence the acceptance of abortion by most and the evolution of gay marriage and recreational pot in the USA today.

# AND WE ARE LEFT WONDERING WHY (in prose)

Did she go hiking alone in the woods, right?
Here is one explanation:
Many years ago, a former Chairman or boss, about
65 at the time, told me he would spend his vacation
in Spain.......running with the bulls. Poor me, just
hearing about the famous, annual, Spanish event
for the first time, asked, what was that about?
He said, to the Spanish, it was about a time-honored
tradition and a boost to tourism but to an old guy like
him, it was about the "matador syndrome".
Oh yes, he went on to explain, that in life there is this
need for some of us to take risks, live on the edge etc.
and that brain which has a high threshold for pleasure
pushes us to do it. And that, that is what the so-called
matador syndrome is about,
Then he listed bull fighting, bungee jumping, sky diving,
mountain climbing, motor car racing, Russian roulette,
running with the bulls etc., as some examples of this
need.
And I guess we can add, women running with "the
wolves" among us, alone in a park or in the woods,
as another example.

# AS THE AURA OF CELEBRITY FADES WITH AGE (in prose)

As the aura of celebrity fades with age, his accusers are emboldened and so the truth rolls off the tip of their once credulous tongues about the dark side of once a "Family Values" Icon now in the twilight of his miserable life.

And how he defiled them in ways, insidious and beastly!

# ASSAD, EXPOSED AS KEEPER OF THE CORRIDOR OF HATE IN SYRIA AND SURVIVAL OF THAT CROCODILE (in prose)

Assad, effectively stripped by the rebels of his WMD, Northern, Eastern and parts of Southern Syria but strongly defended with the help of Russia, Iran and Hezbollah in Central and Western Syria, only exposed him as KEEPER OF THE CORRIDOR OF HATE,
    Damascus,
its suburbs and the region adjacent to Hezbollah in Lebanon. Those are the areas used for the transshipment of deadly weapons from Russia and Iran to Hezbollah and its sidekick, Hamas for attacking Israel.

This corridor was the same place from where lethal gases were catapulted to other areas to kill his own people. This corridor was the same place where Obama's red line was crossed and he had it in the cross hairs for a strike which Putin talked him out of doing.

Oh yes, Obama did spare THAT CROCODILE when he had a chance,
a good reason or excuse to take it out summer 2013. Now it will get stronger, smarter and more costly for Israel or/and another US President to deal with and that they must, in the future.

# AT LAST, HOODIE AGAIN (in prose)

For the first time since Trayvon Martin's killing in February of 2012, I braved donning my hoodie, again today.

Oh, yes, I threw it on for a walk through the neighborhood to see if Christmas had arrived there as yet.

And it sure has, with the decking of hanging, decorative, lighting fixtures on utility poles with images of boughs of holly and jingle bells, with compliments of the City Council, I guess.

By the way, the walk was incident-free.

Fortunately, there wasn't any creepy, crazy, trigger-happy killer doubling as a Neighborhood Watchman, profiling and accosting me as a suspicious character in a hoodie. But in any event, I was prepared for that eventuality and I would have certainly stood my ground.

# BALTIMORE, ANOTHER LIGHTHOUSE (in prose)

Voices wailing in the wind for change and an undercurrent of anger and discontent just turned into a wave and it is growing.
This ship of state must chart different course or sail these troubled waters against a tidal wave of unending unrest.

# BEAUTY PAYS (in prose)

O, how it pays to be beautiful!
Good looks are a priceless
gift from birth, from which the
recipient profits for life.

# BLAME TYRANTS FOR THE TERRORISTS, NOT US (in prose)

One is an outlaw when one practices to
exist outside the law or when one feels
so wronged by the system that one resorts
to unlawful practices as recourse.

These views of course, are in accordance
with Western Values.

But when one exists in a tyrannical State
which itself is a State of lawlessness and
injustice and the only recourse left, is for
one to resort to unlawful practices against
such a State, can one truly be deemed an
outlaw under such conditions?

The answer to that is above my pay grade.

However, we know that when one who feels
wronged by such a State, carries out violent
acts against that State or any other State
allied to that State but is not necessarily
tyrannical too, in order to effect change
and innocent lives are sacrificed by such
acts for such a cause, that person or
outlaw is called a terrorist.

# CHIVALRY, THE GIST (in prose)

There is power in the submissiveness
of the woman and that "submissiveness"
is equal to the "authority" of the man
which makes them equal but different
partners.
But the real difference between them, is
the reflection of the love and care in the
woman, that she receives from the man,
and the security that the man guarantees
in return.

# COMMEMORATING WHAT (in prose)

There is no doubt that for every disaster, natural or otherwise, it is only human to commemorate them in ways that are personal and private, especially the loss of life. And if they disrupted all of our lives like say 9/11, then government would have an interest and a cause in commemorating them for days.

But Katrina, this natural disaster which occurred on George W Bush's watch, I am not sure what we are commemorating. I am not sure whether it is the Act of God, the dead or the "failure" of a President, "a mere mortal ", to stop a natural disaster. This has taken on such a political tone that our kids are bound to be confused about it too.

And all those tornadoes, features of these climatic conditions we live under, who is to blame for those, when they are commemorated?

# CONTROL YOUR DESTINY (in prose)

Control your destiny while you can, for if the past was previously the present and the future is eventually the present, then the present is the defining moment of all times.

# CURBING YOUR ENTHUSIASM (in prose)

A former Chairman, Charles Young, used to remind us whenever something good happens like for example, Trump's change of heart on Syria and his military strike against Assad for gassing people protesting his rule, that "one swallow does not a summer make."

And then there was Churchill in WW11, after a battle has been won, telling the folks, "this is the end of the beginning, not the beginning of the end."

# DESERVING THE LEADER THEY CHOSE, THE CURSE OF THE ILL-GOTTEN (in prose)

A man went to the devil for ill-gotten gain. Ill-gotten because he had to do evil deeds to get it. Then to keep it, he must continue doing more for the devil.

Then the man went to the people for ill-gotten political power. Ill-gotten because he had to lie to get it. Then to keep it, he must keep lying to the people.

Now, The Curse of The Ill-gotten is upon the people.

# DESTITUTE, FOR NOT BEING A MAN (in prose)

He is not a man, if all he has is money and no manners. For manners maketh the man, they say, not money.
And if he is destitute of that which is precious to us, a most cherished value, that makes him Destitute, For Not Being A Man.

# DIFFUSION OF RESPONSIBILITY
## (in prose)

It is spread around so no one person
has it, the responsibility.
We hear our neighbor beating his wife
and so do the other neighbors. But no one
lifts a finger to call the Police or to help,
for each neighbor is expecting another
to do it.
A cat in the neighborhood is clawing the
kids so he needs to be belled. But no one
does it because each is expecting another
to do it.
And then a wild bull on the loose in the
neighborhood needs to be subdued, to
be taken by the horn but by who.
So diffusion of responsibility can be as
much of a problem or even a bigger
problem than the problem itself.

# DOUBTING THOMAS AND THE ARAB SPRING (in prose)

There was a time, a very long
time ago, Doubting Thomas,
no pun intended, asked those
very questions and the rebels,
characterized as, "not freedom
loving", prevailed against their
oppressors.
Now, we live in freedom here
in America.
And how we revere them as
our Founding Fathers.

# EVEN THE DEVIL CITED THE SCRIPTURE FOR HIS OWN EVIL PURPOSE IN BIBLICAL TIME (in prose)

So ISIS corrupting a religion to enslave Muslims is nothing new.

Europeans did, in exchanging the Bible for the land with the Native Americans in 1492 and again on the West coast of Africa as slave merchants cloaked as missionaries and throughout slavery to convert the slaves to Christianity under duress.

Before that they did cite the scripture during the crusades back in the 11th 12th and 13th centuries and Muslim armies used the sword to force the conversion of the infidels, back in the day.

So the ISIS terrorists are merely repeating the history of their forefathers and humanity in a sense.

And war was the antidote as usual.

# GOD, HELP US! (in prose)

We like the mother birds, eager
to see their young ones fly and
feed, are eager to see our babies
walk and talk.
Those early acts of true independence,
the baby steps to a long journey.
And then we navigate the future
with them, with us as their guides.
God, help us!

# GOOD TRY AND GOODBYE
# ASSAD (in prose)

Syria says it would work with any State to
fight ISIS.

Tyranny and terrorism are two heads of the
same monster. Tyranny can rip the soul from
a man and fill his empty vessel up with hatred
for humanity, including himself.

That explains the phenomenon of the suicide-
bomber.

So there is a link between tyrants and terrorists
and that is, the body of the monster and to slay
it both heads must be cut off from the hate-filled
body politic of the Middle East and North Africa.

And that's why I support both the Arab Spring
to oust tyrants like Assad and the War on Terror,
to be consistent.

# GOVERNMENT BY GUNMEN HAS ALWAYS FAILED (in prose)

Never since the beginning of time, a few men armed with guns and forcing millions to do things against their will, sustained, successfully.

Soon the masses will realize that they are controlled by only their own fear of the guns and rise up against them with their own arms or by sabotage, collusion with enemies of the gunmen etc., to free themselves. We saw this with Fascism, Communism, other forms of Tyranny etc. and once again, we will see it with Islamic Fundamentalism.

# HER CONSUMING PASSION (in prose)

As earth welcomed her at birth to life's journey through her
destiny,
her soul visited the dreams of a boy and a man. They would
eventually meet her. First the boy after sixteen years of her journey
and he was consumed by her passion so much and they fell in love,
wedded and started a family. Then the man after twenty five years
of her journey
and he too was consumed by her passion but because she wedded
the boy who was now a man, the older man was mortified but
captivated and so as an unrequited lover, he waited for thirteen
more years,
sharing a destiny with them both, before he was ultimately
devoured
by her passion too. And now she has them both, each a part of her
and her passion is satiated, thus, fulfilling her purpose on earth,
forever.

# HER VIRGIN VOYAGE (in prose)

Hers, a new world, unexplored.
He, an explorer, willing to take
her on a voyage to the unknown,
to uncharted parts to discover
the potentials and tap them.
Tap the youth, the energy and
the innocence for as explorer,
the development of her world
is a way of fulfillment to him
and more importantly, it is the
blooming of her womanhood.

# HOMOSEXUALITY (in prose)

Christians will tell you that the Bible says homosexuality
is a sin. That may be true. But if you believe in God and
that God is the Creator of all human beings and all things
then there is a contradiction since sins are not of God and
homosexuality is in human nature so that will require
some reconciliation.

If you take everything in the Bible literally and without
any doubt, even though it was written by fallible men,
then you won't be able to do that reconciliation and will
be deemed a bigot, rightly or wrongly.

Now, if you are the type that trust in God and do not take
everything in the Bible literally and allow room for possible
errors in translation, the nuances, that which is subject to
interpretation etc., then you will be able to do a reconciliation
of that contradiction and you will come to the conclusion
that God, the only infallible being, who created all of us in
His own image, would not err in creating homosexuals.
Therefore, God is the only arbiter on homosexuality. In other
words, Man or government cannot sit in judgment of
homosexuals.

And once you get to that point, you should come to accept
it even if you don't agree with it.

# HONOR OR TO HONOR (in prose)

Honor Or To Honor is one of the most
important things to Man and they say,
it is even practiced among thieves.
We are taught from birth, to honor our
fathers and mothers.
We show honor to loved ones, family
and friends and to neighbors too.
And we generally, honor agreements,
contracts, treaties and commitments...
This is the common thread that binds
the social fabric together.
Wherever it breaks there is discord.
So you see life would be impossible
without Honor Or To Honor.

# HOW DID THIS HAPPEN? (in prose)

How did a civilized world with its mighty armies equipped with well-trained warriors and great arsenals of smart bombs, drones etc. to defend it, allow Islamic State of Iraq and Syria (ISIS), a band of armed bandits, common criminals, to lay siege to the cradle of civilization? How were they allowed to achieve so much with so little and with such brutality and barbarism in such a world?

# HOW TIMES HAVE CHANGED! (in prose)

Once, warfare was almost private. Fought on battlefields in faraway lands. We only got the results at the end of the war, who won etc.

And Police Brutality used to be a big secret for the Police, let out to the public, occasionally.

Today, details of the atrocities of both are beamed to us in our living rooms by YouTube, smart phones equipped with cameras etc...

And there is no such thing as the fog of war and the occasional Police Brutality, anymore!

# INVISIBLE SHACKLES (in prose)

Fear, the invisible shackles of tyranny,
the enslavement of a whole nation by
an evil ruler who commands his army
to use it to perpetuate his injustice.
And so the greatest weapon against
tyranny is the absence of fear and
the will to die for freedom

# KING OF THE BEASTS (in prose)

The old lion laid down in the jungle, fanning flies with his paws.

The little cubs came nibbling at his ears, playfully.

The monkeys watching from the hilltop and thinking that the old lion is too weak to stop the cubs from interrupting his rest, went to join the cubs to test their theory.

The tigers saw that and they too surmised that the old lion was done, that he was finished being King of The Jungle. So they decided to move in for the kill. The long awaited revolution to make one of them King of The Jungle was, finally, in sight

They charged towards the old lion who was being patient with his grandchildren and even more patient with the monkeys who were really his friends.

The tigers thought they were seeing an opportunity when the old lion sprung up, shuck his mane and let out the roar of his life, heard across the jungle, across the ocean in distant places.

And the tigers retreated in horror as they, the rest of the animals and the people hearing the roar, are reminded that the lion is King of The Beasts.

# LESSER THAN A BEAST (in prose)

And what then is Man,
devoid of compassion,
if not lesser than a beast?
For even a beast is capable
of compassion.
And what if he lacks
compunction too, would
not he be worse? For now
he is without conscience
as well.
That which elevates him.

# LET THE MUSIC PLAY (in prose)

Let The Music Play their
hands caressing their bodies,
each to the other, play the
rhythm of their bodies together,
play the harmony of the beats
of their hearts and of their voices
whispering in their ears, each to
the other, sweet melodies of love
and desire, crescendoing to a
climactic end to their beautiful
dance.

# LET US NOT FOOL OURSELVES (in prose)

The words Christians or Coptic Christians are synonymous with Westerners in the Muslim countries.

Yet past US Administrations and Western Allies thought it a good idea to prop up tyrannies which would bound to hurt the people in Muslim countries, where some are steeped in religious fanaticism and are already disposed to violence by the sword of radical Islam, according to their radical interpretation of Mohammad's teachings, and where Christians are residing for decades.

Such a fringe is bound to fan the flames of vengeance that would soon rise up with popular support in what is now known as the Arab Spring against those tyrants, and curse the Westerners who supported them in the process, hence the backlash against Christians shielded by those ousted tyrants and who were seen as Westerners in those countries, unfortunately.

# LOYALTY (in prose)

Loyalty, that instinctive virtue should
be its own reward, however, when
blindly given to the unworthy, it could
become a liability to the giver, a wrong,
which by its very nature, is a betrayal
of a trust, unfortunately.

# LUSTFUL DREAMS (in prose)

And the lustful are dreamers too.
For only dreamers lust and lust they
must for lust is but a dream.
But some lustful dreams of carnal
bliss leave nothing there to reminisce
and since dreams are not memories
past and these lustful dreams are all
but cast, there is nothing there for
them to last.
Like when those dreams come true.

# MOMENTS (in prose)

There were the best and
the worst of times.

Times of ambivalence,
times to cherish, times to
regret and sometimes
bittersweet.

But times that made me
wiser and stronger.

Moments that are my life.

# MOPES OF A JILTED LOVER (in prose)

And then he exclaimed, what am I, am
I not a man with needs, who dreams, who
feels and who bleeds or am I of the trees!
Cut me with a knife and strike a tree with
the blade of an ax to see which one bleeds!
But then, a tree could fare better than a
man, in the affairs of the heart.
Some trees are nurtured, cared for and loved
as long as they are alive but ironically, here,
a man, who feels treated like a tree, is
really, a jilted lover.

# MUSLIM PEOPLE ARE LIKE RAG DOLLS (in prose)

To Tyrants, Occupiers and Jihadists etc.

These poor people are constantly oppressed and forced to relocate because of tyranny, occupation and terror.

They are to their oppressors as rag dolls are to kids.

# NOTHING IS IMPOSSIBLE (in prose)

Just when you think you have seen
and heard it all, Life shows you that
the impossible can become improbable,
that the improbable can become possible,
that the possible can become probable,
that the probable can become…..well
…..what can I tell you?
That the impossible can happen!

# NOTORIETY, ANOTHER FACE OF EVIL (in prose)

We see the atrocities in the news and they come is all forms, committed by those with the darkest agendas. Some with manifestos of madness attached and others, inexplicable!

Some are one or two-day news and others, recurrent and may disappear from the news in the short or long run.

But one thing remains, we never forget them. They somehow are embedded in our memories, separate and collective, forever.

That is, Notoriety, Another Face of Evil and it has been a facet of humanity for a long, long time.

Shakespeare described it best in this quote: The evil that men do lives after them; the good is oft interred with their bones

# OLD AGE (in prose)

Old Age, that insidious beast, that creeps upon us like a thief in the night, gnaws away at our being, then devours us, completely.

# ONCE MORE (in prose)

Once more we march as life's clock ticks through winter, spring, summer and autumn.
Another year and what's in store, what good and bad fortunes there await.
A slow march, brave soldiers, into the unknown, undaunted, ready to deal with the challenges and greet whatever joy may come.
But determined to get to the next winter no matter what then, Once more…..

# PERSUASION (in prose)

A bigot says something that we don't like and we shame
that bigot into apologizing and that makes us feel good
but the bigot remains a bigot for we failed to persuade
that person's soul to change with logic and facts.
Shaming someone into doing something, is convincing
that person against that person's will and so that person
is left with the same opinion still. You may have heard
that before and is the truth.

Better to change a soul and make that the goal than to
seek to change a will where thoughts remain still, for
fickler than the soul is the mind, known long since, it
was better to persuade than to convince

# POLITICS WITH THE POETIC ORATORY (in prose)

As a young lad with a developing sense of poetry, I was always drawn to politics by politicians who mastered the art of expressing their thoughts and visions while waxing poetic.

Oh yes, I discovered that poetry was the music of mathematics and politics too. Mark you, not all politicians are orators. In fact, to me, most are not. But there are a few who can express themselves on occasions with an interesting choice of words.

The orators I have heard are even fewer, about five so far in my lifetime. And the beauty of this oratory, this poetry, is how the phrases and the flourishes echo through time and space and across generations.

Take Winston Churchill, a former Prime Minister of Britain, our Colonial Masters, he died at 90 in 1965 when I was 14. There was a speech he made in WW11 and the whole world loved it, except of course, the Axis Powers. My parents used to echo these lines from that speech, "we shall fight on the beaches, we shall fight on the landing grounds, we shall fight in the fields and we shall fight in the streets, we shall fight in the hills, we shall never surrender".

Take these lines from John F Kennedy's inaugural address 1961, Actually, this whole speech was a poem, to me that is, "Let both sides seek to invoke the wonders of science instead of its terrors. Together let us explore the stars, conquer the deserts, eradicate disease, tap the ocean depths ... And ***ask not what your country*** can do for you--ask what you can do for your country".

Take these lines from an Address at a special meeting of the General Assembly in observance of the International Anti-Apartheid Year, UN by Michael Manley, Prime Minister of Jamaica, 1978, "Even as I stand here, we feel the presence of the spirit of martyrs who died at Sharpeville and Soweto...... Even as I speak, millions of young lives are being warped and crushed in South Africa, Namibia and Zimbabwe, and their blighted hopes stand as a monumental reproach to all mankind".

Take this line from Ronald Reagan's farewell speech in 1989, "The past few days when I've been at that window upstairs, I've thought a bit of the '***shining city*** upon a ***hill***'. The phrase comes from John Winthrop, who wrote it to describe the America he imagined".

Take this line from Barack Obama's poetry-laced victory speech 2008, on his election as the first black President, "It's the answer that led those who've been told for so long by so many to be cynical and fearful and doubtful about what we can achieve to put their hands on the arc of history and bend it once more toward the hope of a better day'.

And how our Founding Fathers did wax poetic! Take any line of any speech of any Founding Father (politicians in their own right in their time) and see the phrases and flourishes that inspired and lifted us up as a nation, echoing through time and space and across generations, reflected in our National Anthem and the Declaration of Independence.

Now, how we yearn for that Politics With The Poetic Oratory!

# PRINCIPLES OVER POLITICS, ANYTIME! (in prose)

Daily I would come across Ideologues and Partisans and I am beginning to prefer Ideologues. Partisans recite what their Political Parties are saying and they do not think for themselves. They are like sheep bleating whatever, unthinkingly. On the other hand, Ideologues who are just as stubborn and inflexible, at the very least, are about principles, not so much campaigning for the platform or planks of a particular Political Party.

Principles over politics, anytime!

# PUTIN, HERO TO MANY, EVEN IN THE USA (in prose)

Putin is the embodiment of something deep
from inside Russia, the opprobrium felt by
many over the fall of the Soviet Empire in
1991, and you can cut it with a knife. Putin
would say aloud, echo repeatedly, as recently
as when addressing the Russian Parliament
on March 18, 2014, the following.…...........
"The dissolution of the Soviet Union was
the worst tragedy of the 20th Century."

And who do you believe gets blamed for it?
That is why Putin does what he does and
diplomacy and democracy are of no interest
to him. He is seen as some hero to that which
he embodies for holding the handle of the knife
on Iran's developing nuke, stopping the US in
Syria, annexing Crimea, stopping the US plans
for a Missile Defense System in Europe etc.
And as Hero To Many, Even In The USA,
he will only continue down that path until he
is stopped decisively, once and for all.

# RACIAL PROFILING, THAT INSIDIOUS, EVIL THING (in prose)

Racial Profiling is like Sexual Harassment.
And to behold it or hearken a description
of such is to determine whether it was such
and it has an insidious, evil nature so unless
one knows it, such is not easily discernible.

# RIGHT & WRONG, GOOD & BAD (in prose)

What happened to these concepts, whither they went!
We learn about the concepts of right & wrong/good & bad
from our parents and Sunday School first. Then we continue
these lessons throughout our school years, generally but
somewhere between school and on becoming parents, the
lines between right & wrong/good & bad become blurred
for some of us.

Let me offer a couple of examples.

The recent revolts by the Arab people against Tyrants and
their Police States, some the USA propped up for many years,
were sparked by an incident of Police Brutality in the streets
of Tunis, Tunisia, late 2010. That incident set off a chain of
revolutions from Tunisia to Egypt, Libya, Yemen etc. and one
is still raging in Syria at the time of writing.

Police Brutality is a problem here in America too. And recent
incidents, courtesy of smart-phone recordings, sparked protest
across the nation where the Police Brutality is accompanied
by homicides involving unarmed citizens. Police Officers have
been charged in some cases by Public Prosecutors who want
to bring the perpetrators to justice.

Some see nothing right and good in Arab uprisings and these
are the same people who invariably see nothing right and good
in the protest and prosecution of alleged bad cops in America.

And it is no coincidence that most of these people are defenders of the Status Quo and style themselves as ideologically conservative.

My final example is the legalization of pot for recreational use by a few States. We all know how disastrous another legal drug, alcohol, is for our society. Still some of us want another drug, marijuana, legalized for recreational use. These people see nothing wrong and bad about this. And it is no coincidence that most of them style themselves as ideologically liberal.

# SENILITY, BETRAYER OF THE UNCONSCIOUS (in prose)

"As a man thinketh, so is he - Scripture". But will we truly know him, if we don't hear or see some of his thoughts. Those he holds as secrets. Some good, some sinful, some impractical, some unthinkable but thoughts that are his and are a part of him, the unconscious him. Thoughts that never turned to action, forgotten thoughts, buried deep in his unconscious only to be later retrieved and revealed by Senility, Betrayer of The Unconscious. Then suddenly, the man we thought we knew, was not the man we thought we knew.

# SHEEPDOGS (in prose)

Sheepdogs, they protect the herd from the wolves among you. These warriors, trained and dressed as officers of the law, the military, firefighters and the like but they possess the killer-instinct and have a capacity for violence which they use in the defense of justice for you, "the herd".

And what would you do without them, who you take for granted, until you are attacked by "wolves in sheep's clothing". Then you realize how important they are and you call on them to come to your defense, and even when you just "cry wolf", they still come to your defense.

# THAT BAD LIBERAL THING (in prose)

Pushing an agenda under the guise of fairness
or equality, is the way of Liberals.

This is their glorification of bad behavior and
blurring of the difference between right and
wrong through legislation, namely, legalizing
marijuana under the guise of medicine, teaching
sex and homosexuality in school under the
guise of sex education, taking Separation of
Church and State too far except in their efforts
to redefine marriage etc., all while coarsening
society in the process.

The trouble is, the poisonous seed of decadence
always takes root on a slippery slope.

# THAT IS WHO HE IS (in prose)

Now at the age of retirement, his choices are two.
Complacency as a grandfather living in the home
of his son and be Sitter to his grandson or challenge.
The challenge of places to go, people to meet and
goals still to be achieved.
And so he chose the latter for That Is Who He Is,
to choose a path of uncertainty, of disappointments
maybe and even failure too. A potentially difficult
path but one that could make unfinished dreams
come true and new ones too but a path that could
bring even more satisfaction for That Is Who He Is.

# THAT PERVERSE VOICE (in prose)

Be wary of That Perverse Voice
Makes hard what was a simple choice
When what was dark would come to light
Makes up seems down and wrong looks right

# THE AMERICAN (ANTI-FEMINIST) PATRIARCHY (in prose)

The US Presidency is a Patriarchy and it is fiercely, perpetuated by a powerful misogynously-derisive media, a phony-feminist Left (phony because it has a "pro-choice" litmus test, for recognizing and accepting, who is a feminist in its view) and a significant percentage of anti-feminist Right. Cases in point,

Hillary Clinton, Sarah Palin, Michele Bachmann and Carly Fiorina. All four have had aspiration to be President and have been parodied relentlessly, in the media on the Left and on the Right, and unjustifiably so. There was a Newsweek Cover with an image of Michele Bachmann, portrayed as "Crazy", along with the title, "The Queen of Rage", when she ran.

What I am saying, is that a "woman" for President, is not in the psyche of the American people up to this point, who have been so used to hearing about the Founding Fathers and those past male Presidents etc., for such a long time.

Culturally, there is a blindness and a silence for that and it is amplified only in the media with caricatures of women who dare to try.

And the American people are complicit in that by not speaking out against it enough. So what you have is a cycle of perpetual blindness to it and silence to it by the American people. When and if that cycle will break, no one knows but at any rate, maybe not in our lifetime, my friend.

Just some food for thought!

# THE BEAST WITHIN (in prose)

Devoid of any rational thought from hate and fear, they are reduced to The Beast Within, driven by mere adrenaline and the killer instinct. And like a cornered beast they lash out at, claw at and rip to pieces, anyone or anything in their path.

And while they may kill thousands of the innocents in this beastly state, this evil will soon end. For like a cornered beast, they will soon be put down.

Then shackled, taken away and never to be seen again.

# THE CANDIDATE (in prose)

A populist was he but in style more than substance. And buoyed by this populism, he spoke with a forked tongue to diehard constituents so dazzled and blinded by him, they couldn't know the difference. To the general populace, he had no such appeal and there his views were less than palatable. A majority knew that he must be roundly rejected by the ballot, he with his bankrupt ideas must be so humiliated, that his supporters become disillusioned for the greater good...

# THE CYNIC (in prose)

The concept of the circle of life begins with the Fifth Commandment, "Honor thy mother and father" and there is this old saying, "Once a man, twice a child", made popular by the Shakespearean Play, Hamlet, "An old man is twice a child."

We take care of our children when they are young, and as we grow older and weaker, and they grow stronger, they take care of us.

Yet, The Cynic, Clarence Seward Darrow, tells us, "The first half of our lives is ruined by our parents, and the second half, by our children." And now the whys and wherefores are food for thought.

# THE ELUSIVE, KISSING FLOWER (in prose)

A mysterious Mother Nature has done it again.

This time as the romantic.

Springing up amidst the grass, is a flower of rare beauty with petals mimicking lips, pouting kissable lips.

And rarely seen by anyone except he who would nurture it and kiss it from time to time.

# THE HEAD OF THE SPEAR (in prose)

I have this niece, she is in her late teens
and she has signed up to be a Marine.

We are so proud of her!

She is completely, fearless, as brave as
can be.

I am in awe of her courage and character!

So a couple months ago, we got to talking
about her decision. I assured her, that it
takes a special person to want to serve in
the Military of one's country. She quipped,
"And as the head of the spear"!

I asked, what that meant and she explained,
that the Marines lead the way into combat.
They go in first to ensure that it was safe for
Army, the Navy, the Air Force et al, to go
in to the theater of combat.

She compared all of that operation to a spear
and placed the Marines at the head of it. You
see her bravery!

So I asked, why the Military, the Marines.

Lo and behold, she said it has been her life's
dream to join up, to fight for her country, see
the world and achieve the highest rank.

And while the question of getting killed in combat was at the tip of my tongue, she did not give me a chance to ask it.

She was not Pollyannaish in any shape or form! Her goal was to live her dream and I did not sense any preoccupation with death or fear of death, so I focused on her achieving her goal, instead.

I wished her success in her future endeavors.

And you know what, she signed up to be a Marine, The Head Of The Spear. She did not sign up to to be killed!

The brave among us, the members of the Armed Forces, the Fire Brigade, Police Officers, Astronauts etc. will always sign up to serve and that is how we should remember them, as heroes.

# THE INNOCENT CHILD (in prose)

So the innocent child is born in sin. And soon to be given a chance as a soldier for good, in the eternal battle of good versus evil.

Then equipped with the innate weapons of conscience and the free will, and another weapon, religious faith, which is also available but not compulsory, the child enters this life's battle.

The weapon of religious faith comes about through the introduction to the Holy Book about the history of the conflict and the teachings of right and wrong etc.

The goal here is to conquer evil with good to rid one's life of sin.

How well the innate weapons of conscience and the Free will are used, will determine the outcome of the battle for each person. And some find that religious faith increases the odds for victory.

# THE IRAQ WAR, A SHORT STORY (in prose)

Right after 9/11 Bush told us
he feared Saddam would give the
Weapons of Mass Destruction (WMD
the US gave him in the past) my
emphasis, to terrorists.

Most Democrats, Republicans and
Independents agreed with Bush
and encouraged him to get back
the WMD from Saddam. He tried
and Saddam refused to return
them. Then Bush told us he
would have to go and take
them back by force.

Again, the same people agreed
except there was one notable
dissent on this occasion, a
State Senator with Presidential
ambition, Obama, who suggested
that would be a mistake.

However, Bush proceeded with
his plan to invade Iraq 2003
but failed to recover the WMD
immediately and so the war
became mostly unpopular for
that reason together with a
5-year insurgency which saw

the deaths of about 4,000
troops and a huge financial
cost. And still no WMD.

By the time Bush left office
2008 the US had won the war
but he soon handed Iraq over
to the new President, Obama,
to continue the security of
Iraq, generally.

By 2011, Obama decided to give
up the security of Iraq by
withdrawing all combat troops
from that country at once.

In July 2014, this was reported
by the UNITED NATIONS - "Iraq
said the Islamic State extremist
group has taken control of a vast
former chemical weapons facility
northwest of Baghdad, where 2,500
chemical rockets filled with the
deadly nerve agent sarin or their
remnants were stored along with
other chemical warfare agents."

Oh, yes, terrorists found some
of the elusive WMD.

And for the record, the Islamic
State is a terrorist group,
formerly known as Islamic State
of Iraq and the Levant, which
laid siege to Northern Iraq
since June of 2014.

# THE KKK LIVES! (in prose)

Finally, in 2015 once again, this insidious monster rears its ugly head. One Hundred and Fifty four years since its birth and Ninety Four years since its first resurrection for all the world to see and like the phoenix, rises from the ashes of itself, only it had a racist past. And again it uses an immigration crisis as propaganda for new recruits.

Its message, "If it ain't white, it ain't right. White Power." Xenophobic Racists cloaked as "anti-illegal immigration" activists.

More anon!

# THE LAST GASP OF A PATRIARCHY! (in prose)

Did you know that when creatures or entities die a natural death, their deaths result from them attacking themselves?

That when a body is cancer-riddled it is because it enables the cancer to spread throughout, thus destroying itself in the process. That heart attacks are also the body attacking itself and so on and so forth.

That when the Soviet Union fell during the Cold War, there was a lot of internal struggles among comrades before the ultimate collapse.

That fatal, self-inflicted wounds are a reality of life generally, for example, suicide or this could occur within a group of any life form as cannibalism whether real or metaphorically but death or ruin is the result.

One such entity is The American "Anti-Feminist" Patriarchy of 240 years. We are now witnessing on the Right of it, some chasmal, political infighting, as a strong woman from the Left waits in the wings as it falters then fades, with her as its first woman President.

But will it?

# THE LONE KAYAKER (in prose)

Out there, The lone kayaker, adrift in the deep blue when the sun peers through the dark clouds for her to embrace its warm rays, to keep her company. And at the horizon, she kissed the rays goodbye, then paddled back in the twilight as the moon smiled down at her as her new companion.

She'd soon be home away from flirting with Mother Nature.

Now, awakened from a dream, cuddled in the arms of her lover fast asleep beside her, she realized that her as The Lone Kayaker, was just a wet dream.

# THE MAN CAVE (in prose)

Now into The Man Cave where she
puts him. That last bastion of
masculinity? Oh no!
That glorified doghouse, no longer
on the living room couch but into the
basement, with all the amenities, a
bed, a stove, a washing machine,
a drier etc.
All the things to his comfort but her.
A fate worse than that of a caveman,
since even he had his woman in his
cave.

# THE NEW TERROR ARMY, ISIS, WINNING THE WAR ON TERROR? (in prose)

The world had become so desensitized to the savagery of Al Qaeda in Iraq under Zarqawi before he was slain by US troops. Then, his band of terrorists spawned or inspired by The Bin Laden Al Qaeda, was mostly crushed by the Surge in 2007 but some disappeared underground.

That was the first defeat of The Bin Laden Al Qaeda since it attacked the US on 9/11/2001. The second defeat was in May 2011 with the killing of Bin laden, same year of the rebirth of Al Qaeda in Iraq into The New Terror Army, ISIS when it joined the rebellion against Assad in Syria.

By the following year, 9/11/2012 The Bin Laden Al Qaeda affiliates in Benghazi attacked the US embassy and killed the US Ambassador and four staff members in Libya and I have learned that some of the killers turned up in Syria as new recruits for ISIS.

Today, ISIS manned by terrorists, spawned or inspired by The Bin Laden Al Qaeda, under a new leader, Baghdadi, is wreaking havoc in Eastern Syria and Western Iraq and carving out a Caliphate from territories formerly known as Syria and Iraq. Iraq where US blood and treasure were spent to defeat The Bin Laden Al Qaeda, its first victory against the group after the 9/11/2001 attack.

And although The Bin Laden Al Qaeda has publicly disowned ISIS because of its savagery, the establishment of the Caliphate is at least seen by Jihadists around the world as a major victory and it serves as a recruiting tool.

Thus the world has come full circle in the War on Terror back to Iraq and it stands by numb to the savagery of The New Terror Army, ISIS, almost resigned to it!

# THE OUTSIDER (in prose)

aka, The "Tinsel Hair" Ogre

Now in charge of a city, he once decried as
broken and its insiders as stupid, for causing
it to lose its sheen as the shining city on a
hill, he risks becoming an insider himself.
And so he set out to drain the swamp as
promised and make the city shine, again!
Soon, to find himself refilling vacancies,
"the swamp" of "the broken city", with
some of the same muck, "stupid insiders"!
But it is still early and we were urged by a
vanquished foe, The Teflon Lady, with the
popular majority, to keep an open mind here,
he deserved it, she said, of The Outsider.

# THE REINCARNATION OF EVIL
# AND ASSAD (in prose)

Ever since Mankind disobeyed GOD and ate the forbidden fruit
from the Garden of Eden, evil came into existence.

As a part of the punishment GOD made evil indestructible and
so it lives forever in Man assuming a different host or multiple hosts
from time to time but still as the original evil.

One can read history to see the litany of those who hosted evil and
their evil deeds.

Hitler for example, was once a host and he manifested evil through
the Nazi Holocaust of the Jews.

And then there were those hosts of evil, manifested through Slavery
and Apartheid.

Today we see evil in the form of tyranny and terrorism around globe,
manifestations of the same original evil.

And there is Assad, another tyrant like Hitler. His hosting of evil and
his evil deeds will be on display in a Museum somewhere. A pictorial
of his systematic extermination through torture and other means, of
hundreds of Sunni people who dared to dissent from his tyrannical
rule in Syria.

And soon evil will find another host or other hosts and there will be
other manifestations of evil but still as the original evil.

# THE RISE, THEN FALL, AS THE CRUSADER (in prose)

Once admired by almost everyone as the capitalist and entertainer, he then turns to politics and things changed.

As the fledgling, aspiring politician, that turns him into The Crusader who grimaces but with anger, as he seldom smiles again.

And he speaks with a fork tongue, methinks, to those from foreign lands and to those he panders to, as The Crusader against political refugees in dire straits and illegal immigrants, who critics say he employed in his real estate endeavors etc., at times past.

And now he is admired by fewer of the almost everyone who used to admire him.

# THE SCOURGE OF TYRANNY (in prose)

Like I said earlier, tyranny has no conscience.

Take a look back on history and see which
Governments bomb their own people and
infrastructure. You will no doubt find that
only tyrannical regimes do this self-inflicted
violence.
All to suppress individual freedoms and crush
the human spirit so to keep millions as slaves
of tyranny under the vicious control of an elite
minority headed by a despot as happens in
Cuba, Syria, North Korea etc.
Any movement or warfare to end this scourge
ought to be supported by the rest of us for
there is no greater wrong known to Man in
this, the 21st. century.
Even slavery was abolished centuries ago
while the scourge of tyranny remains a
cancer in all of humanity.

# THE STATUS QUO AND THE POLICE (in prose)

There is a social bloc of whites, mostly on the Right, I am talking white conservatives, who want the status quo remain, the white supremacy. And there are some on the Left, socially conservative but fiscally liberal, with that mindset too. This is manifested in their blind support for the Police. This blind support for the Police is common ground for this bloc. I have been saying this in several blogs, that the Police is an arm of the State, the original State, the white supremacy. That State is personified by the "white cop" majority and some black cops too (by the way, blacks used to own slaves too). This bloc wants the government to preserve this arm of the State (The Police). And the Grand Jury system which was a tool used by monarchs to strengthen their grip on the State, is the same system the government employs today to protect the Police, thus keeping in place at least, this aspect of the status quo. This bloc refers to blacks as thugs and the Police do the same. I understand from a couple of white ex-cops, who confessed to it, that the use of the phrase "thug" is widely used by the Police as a kind of racial slur. And if you are attentive you would see it used a lot on social media when discussing the Police shootings of unarmed black men. So the epidemic of Police shootings of unarmed black men,
is incidental to the greater issue of preserving the status quo, the white supremacy, insidiously.

# THE TIME HE DISCOVERED HE HAD A CRAZY HAITIAN WIFE (in prose)

This was 1982, three years after they were married. His son was a few months old and still used a crib. One night he came home late from work and found the house in complete darkness. He knew it wasn't a power cut because the neighbors had light and he knew the electric company didn't turn it off because he paid the bill.

So he went outside to his car, got a flashlight and went back inside to check if the baby was in the crib, he was and then he checked the bed to see if his wife was there, she was and she had a long kitchen knife in her hand, ready to slaughter him in the dark.

He didn't have time to find out why so in total shock, he turned off the flashlight and ran towards the front door and she went after him. As soon as he reached the door and opened it, he heard a bang in the door behind him. That sounded like she threw the knife at him, she did. He kept running, passed his car up the long driveway.

He heard footsteps gaining on him, then suddenly they stopped and he stopped too. Then he could hear her in the dark, using the knife toscrap the car's body, hitting the windshield, bursting the tires etc., frantically, like a crazy person.

He left on foot to go to his sister's that night, while leaving his very angry wife doing what she was doing. He stayed at his sister's until the next day and until he could brave it back home later that day

She was now calm when he arrived home. He asked her what was that all about and she kept silent. Then he realized that she had removed all the bulbs from the sockets to leave the house in darkness that night.

Anyway, absent any explanation from her and now afraid of her and for his son, he figured it would be best for them to separate for a while until they figured out what was wrong So he immediately booked a flight for her to Haiti and she agreed to go if their son would go with her. But she still seemed oblivious to what went on the night before as she welcomed the opportunity to go home to Haiti to be with her family again.

So she went and he would follow soon for a visit himself. While in Haiti, he asked again, what was the anger about back in Trinidad. Now, she explained that a friend of theirs, a woman, told her that she saw him driving a woman in his car every morning to work or someplace, for months. And that they look like they were enjoying each other's company. She said after the friend told her that, she only saw darkness like in a blind rage, until she heard about the trip to Haiti.

Then he explained to her that the friend was correct about what she saw but that the friend did something really evil, in telling her about what she saw without at least, finding out from him first, about what was going on etc. And then he told her, the woman in the car was his Secretary, who he picked up for work, from her home, in the mornings.

Anyway, he made her stay in Haiti for fifteen months to make sure that the whole incident was behind them, before allowing her to return home... And they never spoke to the friend again.

Years after that, around the middle of the 1990's, something happened again, involving another woman. But this time, it was a jealous "Policeman" boyfriend who found out that his girlfriend was seeing him socially, as a married man, according to the boyfriend. But she was really, involved in his music business as the manager of his biggest artist at the time so it was really a professional relationship.

Anyway, the boyfriend did some investigation and found out where he lived etc. and went there to report him to his Crazy Haitian Wife.

That set off a series of actions on her part that forced him to spend money faster than he was making it, on the home budget, the kids etc.
A mush longer story!

And that was why she eventually, ended up in America since 1998. he followed eight years later and the rest is history.

Today, the investments he left behind in Trinidad have multiplied to a point where he can return home, fortunately.

He has had his share of a Crazy Haitian Wife, he told his friends!

# THE WOOL BEEN CAST OFF (in prose)

You been had, suckered, bamboozled,
took - Malcolm X (50 years ago).

But no longer my brethren, no more!
The wool been cast off from the eyes,
so that eyes may see clearly now.

# THINGS (in prose)

That we have and that we desire to have,
how they possess us, and we worship them
and give life to these lifeless objects which
are oftentimes, the bones of contention.
We live with them until we die, for they can
and will outlast us, and they usually do. We
even repair and renew them so that they may
last forever and they do, sometimes.
They too want to live and survive, as auntie
Hopie would say, cynically, and if we have
to part with them, willingly or by force, how
it hurts at times.
We clutch and cuddle them, irrationally, as
we grow older, even more than people,
sometimes.
And to what end, for we must part with
them since we can't take them to the grave.
How pathetic!

# THIS FBI PHILOSOPHY (in prose)

Not seeing the world through sides:-

The Director, "We don't see the world that way," he added. "We are not on any-body's side. We really don't care. We're trying to figure out what's true, what's fair, that's the right thing to do."

We could describe it as having a FBI opinion about something or taking a FBI position on an issue or that something is the FBI truth.

# THOSE WISE MEN (in prose)

The Founding Fathers realized that
dealing with Mother Nature was above
their pay grade, and so they left Nature
to run her course.
And that is the reason the Constitution
made no reference to, when personhood
begins, abortion, euthanasia, homosexuality
etc., all matters to be dealt with by
adjudication now, and yet imperfectly so.
Adjudication, the last refuge of the
inconceivable!

# TRUE LOVE (in prose)

In Chinese philosophy, this is a yin
and yang of nature. And in general,
it is the constant reciprocity of need
and supply. A cycle of erotic desires
and slaking, the fountain for renewal
of harmonious, spiritual togetherness.
A mutual appreciation of sharing and
sacrifice. All of which could go on,
forever.

# TYRANNY (in prose)

That modern form
of slavery, a systemic
terrorization and torture
of its own people by a
State, destined to be met
by a bloodless coup or
a violent revolution.

# VICE (in prose)

Vice, the opposite of virtue and, are
the Seven Deadly Sins, Wrath, Greed,
Sloth, Pride, Lust, Envy and Gluttony.
The vicious seven befall Man since the
beginning of time.
And there is no escaping them, unless
he is born again and even then, there
is no guarantee because of the frailties
of Man.
That is how deadly they are and it
makes no difference, if only one of the
seven befalls someone. For the presence
of vice in any form, is enough to drive
someone to wrongdoing and possible
demise.
So that, a purging of all vice from the
soul of Man, is his only salvation

# WHAT DO THEY EXPECT, SHE IS THE TEFLON LADY! (in prose)

Now they say she is "playing with fire" by backing
a recount of the votes in some States, by a Third Party
candidate.

They have failed to burn her at the stake with their
witch hunt for 30 years. So "playing with fire" is
something she does well!

When she conceded to Trump, her right to a recount
was still reserved. And no amount of threats to further
search this Lady's "electronic handbag" for email etc.,
by men from Wikileaks, from Russia and those of The
American (Anti-Feminist) Patriarchy, including, Trump's
veiled threat to appoint a Special Prosecutor, another
male, you bet, to do more searching of her "handbag"
etc. will deter her.

And with all the hacking and invasion of this Lady's
privacy during the campaign, who knows to what
lengths those men when to stop her run!.

She ought to find out and furthermore, she has the
support of a majority of the America people, based
on the results of the election, with her win over
Trump for the popular vote.

# WHEN ANTICIPATION WAS HAPPINESS (in prose)

Thanks for sharing with me, that bit of anticipation that felt like anxiety, my dear Betrothed, said the poet to the bride-to-be. That was really happiness cloaked as anxiety and it shall soon to be uncloaked, That will be your wedding day.

So is happiness always about anticipation, she asked.

Oh no, only when it is anticipation about something wonderful like your marriage, for example. He continues, happiness is a state of mind, they say, different things to different people. And remember this, my dear Betrothed. That tingling thought, the thrill, the trust, the tying of the two, you and your Betrothed. That is happiness to you!

To live along, to learn to love a lot after "I do", you and your Beloved. That is happiness to you!

# WHEN DOUBTFULNESS BECOMES STUBBORNNESS THAT CAN KILL (in prose)

A big killer of the old, is stubbornness. They are as stubborn as the children they once were or worse.

As the old adage goes, once a man twice a child!

This stubbornness is a part of their life's cycle.

First, as children, they are stubborn. Then, to paraphrase the poet, Oscar Wilde, as youngsters, they believe they know everything, at middle age, they soon find out that there are some things they do not know and as they become older, they begin to doubt everything.

That doubtfulness becomes stubbornness that can kill, sometimes.

My big sister, Hopie, once told me that God does have a sense of humor and how He gave us some things for His amusement. Take sex for example, she continued, He
must be amused to see what people would do to have it.

And here am I now, wondering, if it amuses Him to see how all His children cope with stubbornness, as they grow older.

# WHEN LOVE WAS A PRISON (n prose)

Newt and Pansy were two inmates (lovers)
in the prison of love, fifty years to life without
the possibility of parole. But the two were in
separate confinements (marriages) out of sight
and out of touch, an untold punishment.

But after fifty years they were released from
confinements and were still inmates of love,
to finish life without the possibility of parole.

# WHY WE ARE HERE (in prose)

Basically, we are here because
nature requires us to be keepers
of the next generation.
In other words, we are required to
procreate as humans and as parents,
to nurture and protect our young
until they are able to do that for
themselves.
Then they will become keepers
of the next generation that follow
theirs and so on and so forth
Obviously, longevity may make
our keeping responsibility extend
beyond the next generation,
Then we become grandparents,
great-grandparents etc.
And we are required to worship
God, thus perpetually, thanking
God for our existence etc.

# WONDERS, TRULY NEVER CEASE (in prose)

The first time he introduced the notion of, and the meaning of chivalry to his daughter, she was only 16. She scoffed at that notion and laughed at him, saying, "my friends told me that whenever your boyfriend beats you and roughs you up, it is a man's way of showing affection to women. " He said, what? And she continued, "boys who are not like that, are sissies, they say."

He had learned about chivalry from as early as high school, studying English Literature, Shakespearean plays, reading poetry, attending art films with his older sister, who invited him, and who is also a great admirer of chivalrous men. And his impression from all that was, the heroes and/or protagonists, were always, the chivalrous.

So he told his daughter, back then, that she was just simply wrong and suggested that she keeps an open mind about this chivalry thing.

Now, at age 24, she told him, that she has this new boyfriend, who is very spiritual, he reads the Bible and fashions his life off the scripture. He said, seriously? She said, "sure and he shows me chapters, verses, in the Bible about how a man should treat woman, yes daddy,

lessons of chivalry are in the Bible." He didn't
realize that but he didn't act too surprised.
Then it dawned on him that, wonders, truly
never cease.

# YOUR MEMORY (in prose)

And when in the twilight of your life,
may negative memories be forgotten
and the good ones remembered, for
the sake of your grandchildren.
For went you share your memories
with them, you wouldn't want their
little vessels be filled with negativity
by Your Memory, at that tender age.

# Poems

# A BECKONING HAND

Hey dream-maker, tell us this dream
So what it means, what does it seem
A Beckoning Hand gives the creeps
On a winter's night while he sleeps

'twas in this dream about his wife
Whom he loves for half his life
Now awake, he laments his fear
As she assures, she's going nowhere

# A CALL TO POETS

Take up those pens and write
And write with all your might
Let the people's voice be heard
Stroke by stroke and word for word
Express the cause of their unrest
For there's no change without protest
Your rhyme and reason from the heart
Put down in words to show your part

# A FLEETING BEAUTY

Snowflakes early morning
came raining down on me
Snow-white so bright, a
beautiful sight to see

Snowfall then rainfall so
fleeting are the two
All gone by daybreak when
they became the dew

# A JEALOUS MOON

Out here on the Milky Way, the once
bright stars go dark
When a sad moon would cry tonight
when lovers hit the park

The man in the moon joins a flight
of angels for a song
A Jealous Moon would spoil the night,
she takes that as a wrong

Her sadness dims the distant spheres
that matter from afar
So lovers' wishes won't come true
tonight, upon a star

# A LASTING FLAME

After all those moons and other men
She carried a flame from way back when
From over forty years ago
For ex lover who did not know
Now then when he was sixty six
She had a chance to tell him this
But she was free and she has got
A Lasting Flame and empty cot
When she was bold and he was not
And he felt old when she was hot

# A LITTLE BOY & THREE ANGELS

A Little Boy & Three Angels, another
great tale to tell
Who took him on an early start in a life
that turned out well
One taught him how to talk and read,
she saw him twice a day
And one, how to sing and dance and
she taught him how to pray
The third, she was to make sure that
the lad was catching on
For the three were sent by God, Himself,
who smiled upon this one

# A SHAKEN FAITH O LORD

Lord, time and time and time again,
we have to question you
We've seen the work of evil men,
difficult to undo

There're times when that evil deed
is dealt in your name
And A Shaken Faith O Lord, will
never be the same

# A TALE OF TERROR

Grumbling gremlins and a trog
Wreaking havoc in the fog
And that trog, a leader, was
Others mimic what he does
The wretched deeds, one could tell
Are done by creatures out of hell
With evil eyes and huge, long teeth
They took their mischief to the street
Scaring kids and parents too
Spawn them nightmares, that they do

Then darkness comes upon the land
Eyes aflame and knife in hand
They slash the tires of the cars
While drivers mingle in the bars
And all night long, through the towns
Shatter windshields, on their rounds
By daybreak folks had, had enough
Armed with guns and other stuff
Shot those gremlins, end their game
Sent them back to whence they came

# A TRAGEDY WE GRIEVE

They're here today and gone tomorrow
Leaving behind such pain and sorrow
Then we cry an ocean full of tears
Grieving those loved ones through the years

And when those loved ones are our kids
We question how and why that is
A Tragedy We Grieve, what a loss
When our kids should outlive us

# A WONDERFUL, GLORIOUS REVERIE

She lifts up her eyes to see where you are
And there she was being carried by a star
Across the Milky Way, through and through
Closer to heaven, closer to you

And what a flight of fancy it would be
A Wonderful, Glorious Reverie
Across the Milky Way, through and through
Closer to heaven, closer to you

# AFTER THE STORM

Dams are full, no rain to fall
No clouds to form After The Storm
The sea subsides, no life lost
Winds disperse, it could be worse
Roofless homes, flooded fields
The fallen trees, no buzzing bees
New butterflies, no marching ants
A sunny sky, no birds to fly
Schools are out, starry nights
Children play and parents pray
Power outage, lovers love this
Candlelight into the night
One week passed, the city's back
Changing gear, the centers clear

# AFTER THIS WINTER

For ten long years he had these dreams
Where it is cold but summer steams
Nine winters came and then they went
With just a dream until the tenth

After This Winter come the fun
The sea, the sand and lots of sun
Where the music plays night and day
Somewhere, four thousand miles away

# ALL TYRANNY BY THE WEAK

That slaver who had seized his
prey and shackled them to a ship
That brutal despot taking lives
from a fear of losing grip
That sexual predator we can see
and the millions more unseen
That schoolyard bully who can't
control an impulse to be mean
That miscreant with some evil
scheme for ripping off the poor
That terrorist who must use our
fears to force our hand and more
That offspring who would scam
a dad of the little that he had
That lack of conscience that we
see should make us all so sad

# ALLEGORY OF TOWN OF KOBANI

A dark creature came to take the town
And the eagle soared and put it down
Again it tried, it always persists
Battle it will for an oasis
Again and again the eagle soared
But the dark creature will not be floored
They did battle for days day and night
Then the eagle soared with all her might
Too much for dark creature and so it fell
Town of Kobani, its portal to hell

# AMBIGUOUS AMBIVALENCE

Hard to forget, hard to regret,
impossible to undo
Some things we wish we never did
but still relish, they came true
Ambiguous Ambivalence, call it that,
if we must
Never cry over spilled milk or what's
done in faith and trust

Hard to forget, hard to regret,
never a chance to redo
Those things we wish we never did
but still relish, they came true
Ambiguous Ambivalence, call it that,
if we must
Life's too short to worry over what's
done in faith and trust

# AMERICA'S NIGHTMARE

A "tinsel-hair" ogre comes
to town
And turns her cities upside
down
By stoking flames of angry
souls
Make beasts of them to
further goals
When millions saw his evil
ruse
Some pinned their hopes on
one name, Cruz
How longer would this
Nightmare last
Please wake her up when
it has passed

# AN ALLEGORY OF REDEMPTION

Suddenly, the earth ate the trees
Then set out to drink the seas
And after we die as we must
What then of Man reduced to dust
That Judgment Day was imminent
But no one quite knew how it went
Souls awakened in heaven's bliss
Others wept in a dark abyss
Those adrift in purgatory
Still could choose to get the glory

# ANOTHER DAY BUT THE SAME

Old sun rears its big, round head to signal
the break of day
Makers crank their factories up and some
make bricks of clay
Workers stream into streets in obedience
to job rules
As parents dress their children up to send
them off to schools
Consumers make their way to stores with
wads of hard-earned dough
A city comes to life again with commuting
to and fro
Then evening comes along with dusk to
usher in the night
And old sun ducks its head once more to
give way to moonlight
That time for rest is here again, that time
for lover too
Time for sleepers to dream again and
wish some dreams come true

# AUTUMN

Summer winds' butterfly kisses,
bidding us goodbye
Gusting winds, cold and dry,
that time of year draws nigh

# AUTUMN LOOMS

O, so sweet, a friendly breeze
Tickles at your bare-skinned knees
Hear the whispers as it nears
Then it's cooing in your ears
How it woos the swaying trees
Wary of a summer's tease
And their sorrow as it zooms
All telltales that Autumn Looms

# BALLAD OF A SEX ADDICT

He started out, a peeping-tom
and now he has this greed

That'd escalate to masturbate,
by a mind devoid of heed

This voyeur slaves and his
fetish craves but couldn't fill
his need

A chronic weakness for
the flesh, would drive his
sinful deed

# BALLAD OF BEAN COUNTERS

(Inspired by my son and grandson)

Teach them to count on their fingers and toes
The eyes, the ears, the mouth and the nose
They'll be bean counters before they could show
Now watch them spring and watch them glow

# BALLAD OF GO BOMB THE EVIL BANDITS

Go bomb the evil bandits.
bomb them good
Go bomb the evil bandits,
as you should

They captured women on
the mountain top
To sell them into slavery,
make them stop

And save their young sons,
seized against their will
Brainwashed by bandits
and taught how to kill

Go bomb the evil bandits,
bomb them good
Go bomb the evil bandits,
as you should

Rescue those people on the
mountain top
And the evil bandits, make
them pop

They hijacked Islam,
committing their crimes
Then committing each act
numerous times

Go bomb the evil bandits,
bomb them good
Go bomb the evil bandits.
as you should

# BALLAD OF NEW COW WAS OLD COW

Old bull is the sole bull living
on a farm
And he fathers all the cows and
calves, that old charm
But only one per cow and so he
would rule
Memorizing the scent of each, old
bull was no fool

Sniffing through the herd, he finds
unfamiliar scent
Tricky old cow had new cows
licking her at length
Old bull gets ready to be father
once more
But soon to find out the old cow
from next door

# BALLAD OF THAT CELTIC THING

Then in a dream on this glorious night
One sweet angel in a hovering flight
With curly blond hair and bright blue eyes
A hot Celtic woman was in disguise

And he loves to hear her sing

Those sultry songs she did for his treat
In enchanting lyrics and a voice so sweet
He'd soon realize, she is his Muse
And she's the one that he would choose

For he loves that Celtic thing

# BALLAD OF THE EMANUEL NINE

Murdered by Supremist in a Church down south
Martyred over a flag and change came 'bout
Mourned by a nation still healing from the past
God bless the day that flag was taken from the mast

# BALLAD OF THE GAMBLER

He rolled that dice more than once
More than twice he took a chance
Then like a hook, he got caught
He got took, came up with naught
Yet once more he rolled that dice
More than once then more than twice
He rolled that dice just for fun
Tables turned, for now he won

# BALLAD OF THE HITMAN

We saw his targets after they fell
But how he did it, we cannot tell
Wicked men hired him for a plan
To silence opponents by hitman

The lives of saints or the lives of snakes
To a hitman, what difference that makes
His heart of stone paid for in gold
Hired by them, who are just as cold

# BALLAD OF THE PONTIFF

A world against brutality
Let's make it a reality
A world against brutality
Let's make it a reality

Said the man from Rome
Charity begins at home
Send the children to school
Let them learn The Golden Rule
World leaders should have a heart
And they should play their part
To end Police Brutality
And political hostility

A world against abuse
Be truthful with the news
End the tribal war
And the reason that they spar
Let us teach the youth
Not to be a brute
That we shouldn't have to fight
But sometimes might is right

A world against brutality
Let's make it a reality
A world against brutality
Let's make it a reality

# BALLAD OF THE STUNTMAN

Never just a death-defying feat
Or just another daredevil's treat
He dances in the shadows of death
Every time he hits that set

More than a matador's pluck
Or just a gamble on luc
He dances in the shadows of death
Every time he hits that set

No fanciful death-wish dream
Or just another tricky scheme
He dances in the shadows of death
Every time he hits that set

Not a dangerous game of chance
Nor for him, a reckless dance
He dances in the shadows of death
Every time he hits that set

# BALLAD OF THE SURFER

Dazzled, not a dream or reverie
Most beautiful dance you'll ever see
Too far to hear but you see her glides
The roar of the waves on which she rides

On the rhythm of that tidal wave
Her balancing act was all but brave
Surfing the ocean from side to side
A daring dance on a surging tide

The watercraft of amazing feet
Her fleeting moves so nimble and sweet
And when she finally comes ashore
That finds them craving her encore

# BALLAD OF THE TANTRA DANCE

What a leap of faith to fall in love
to do the tantra dance
And what a way, to woo and coo and
cuddle in this romance

Then how to tell the love from lust
when smitten in this trance
If even once for just a chance
to do the tantra dance

# BALLAD OF TWO WRETCHED SOULS

Hearken! This tale of a tragedy about
two wretched souls
One, a wayward youth it seemed to
the other doing patrols

The youth, then stalked by a shadow
of Death on that moonlit night
Like a cornered beast, he pounced on
it but only out of fright

Now how to tell him, his brave attempt
was but a futile leap
When Death's shadow was a gun, in
the hand of a manic creep

But that manic creep did not intend to
shoot that youth to death
And his senseless provocation was
neither ruled a threat

And after all been said and done, only
two would know the truth
One of them, that manic creep and the
other one, that dead youth

So went the tale of a tragedy about
two wretched souls
One, a wayward youth it seemed to
the other doing patrols

# BALLAD OF WHAT IS TO BE

And how this century witnessing a trend
Tyrants and terrorists meeting their end

Old enemies unite with common goals
Battling evil and protecting souls

But for all the good that would obtain
Our world apart, what evil remain

And still in the balance, what is to be
After millions freed of tyranny

May the righteous rules in this campaign
And the martyred souls not fall in vain

# BART, TESS AND THE WIND

She feels his passion in the wind
and he could feel hers too
He sings her love songs in the wind
and she could hear them woo
She blows a kiss into the wind, it
finds the one he blew
And he hears her whisper in the
wind, I love you

# BATTLES OF CIVIL DISOBEDIENCE

No stick, no stone, no more threat
Save those words and save your breath
Get that authorizing slip
Before embarking on a trip
March uptown and march downtown
Keep those feet upon the groun"
Do those battles, wit to wit
When they stand, you choose to sit
Peacefully and better that
Could escalate with tit for tat
Have no fear it is your right
Secured by your forefathers' fight

# BEAUTIFUL HUMMINGBIRD

The most wonderful little
bird that one sees
With fluttering wings that
hum like bees
It hovers in midair on a
nectar search
Just resting there on an
invisible perch
Nature's only creature to
do this, of course
And when, lo and behold,
it flies backwards
Then its trailing tail of
thin black streamers
Would hum us a tune,
fitting for dreamers

# BITTERSWEET MOTHER NATURE

Missing the fluttering butterflies, some
sights and sounds not heard
The wind-dance of the daffodils and the
singing of a bird
He has not seen a rainbow or a flash of
lightning too
Those towering skyscrapers deprive him
of that view
Can hardly hear the thunder, can hardly
hear the rain
Got to keep those windows shut for heat
and cold, the twain
Bittersweet Mother Nature's four seasons
here to stay
Returning to her sights and sounds, he
can't await the day

# BRAIN-SNATCHER

O wonderful Brain-snatcher, how
you're on my mind
And you're such a rarity, that's so
hard to find

You have that look of passion,
your brain-snatching gaze
Beauty that craves attention, your
eye-catching ways

You're so warm and open and
that's interesting and cute
Possessing a free spirit that's
infectious, to boot

# CHANT FOR CHANGE

Let's throw the liars out
To bring that change about
Along with their crooked schemes
And secure our children's dreams

Let's throw the liars out
To bring that change about
Accepting the wrong you know
Enables the status quo

Let's throw the liars out
To bring that change about
You stand up for what's right
And never give up that fight

Let's throw the liars out
To bring that change about
To bring that change about
Let's throw the liars out

# CHIVALRY STILL ALIVE!

Saw Chivalry today with a rose in hand
Waving that rose at women he'd see
He was just three feet tall, toddling the land
And by his toddle, was younger than three

# DEMENTIA, YE OLD DEMON

Dementia, Ye Old Demon, give those
souls a break
Demented and wretched, how much
could one soul take
And what a horrible duo, the two of
then would make
Misery is hard enough, then to suffer
being a flake
Dementia, Ye Old Demon, give those
souls a break

# DESIRE

It feasts the mind to survive
Then whence would it derive
This must be where angels dwell
We're kept under its constant spell
Our lustful eyes are always waked
Our appetites are never slaked
How we grovel with this Desire
Anything to quench that fire
And do not expect it to relent
Until all we can spend, is spent

# EARTH TO MAN

So whence ye came and who'd know
I bring thee, winds and rain and snow
The moon at night when day is done
And stay in orbit of the sun
Just serving nature, duty-bound
Was never flat, was always round
Intriguing design of whose plan
But not of thee, O, puny Man
Ye art mere creatures of the dirt
When ye art gone I'll still be Earth

# ENTERPRISE

When dreamers dream
each dream, anew
And the planners plan
and take risk too
Those dreams, fulfilled,
by coming true
Our lives, improved
because they do

# ESSENCE OF LIFE

Atop Life's mysteries and strife
We're granted the breath of life
That in the happiness we seek
Pray the Lord our soul to keep

Though we're assigned a gender
We're one body in the Maker
That we're our brother's keeper
And destined to meet Grim Reaper

# EVIL AND THE UNEASY HEAD

Evil dressed and masked in creed
It hides behind to do its deed
Made it so you couldn't tell
This coward comes here straight from hell
On whose, the plan to put it down
Uneasy head, that wears a crown
Degrade, destroy to the endgame
Then back to hell to whence it came

# FLAME-ARROWS

How Venus fills her mission
to satisfy Desire
Our souls are filled with passion,
our hearts are set on fire

And when that Eros starts, those
arrows found their marks
Flame-arrows to our hearts,
ignite that love with sparks

# FOR THAT SAME LOVE

And when we pray, our faith is kept
For That Same Love, when Jesus wept
Upon the cross, he took a chance
To save our souls and what a stance
For us to cleanse ourselves of sin
Come heaven's gate, we shall get in

# FOR WHAT GOOD THEN IS LIFE!

For What Good Then Is Life,
if not to feel alive
To see birds build a nest and
bees, to build a hive
To see the sparkling dewdrops
against the rays of the sun
To track a rainbow across the sky
and do it just for fun
To do good deeds when not for pay
only to lend a hand
To be avid for truth and cause or
at least, tell where you stand
To be lucky to be in love and do
what lovers do
To chase those dreams that are
good and hope that they come true
To see a beautiful sunset and too,
the Milky Way
And to wish upon a star to see
another day

# FOREVER, SLAVES

To cracking whips and bound to ships,
they lift the oars to row
Then push and pull, push and pull,
ten thousand miles to go

The cargo breathes and too it bleeds,
in doldrums down below
From hurricanes and sunny clime
to winter storms and snow

All shackled still against their will,
they made plantations grow
Some future kin still pay a price
despite the seeds they sow

# FREDDIE GRAY, A MARTYR MADE

A simple man and O, so sad
Dragged to death by a dark, blue squad
And was no hero to the date
A million marched against the State
For equal rights, they took a stand
And demanded justice in the land
Now, Freddie Gray, A Martyr Made
By foolish men whose light shall fade

# GARGOYLES

Monsters of the dark, they
sleep by day
Perched on buildings even
where we pray
Scary winged creatures, they
fly by night
In dreams of kids, paralyzed
by fright
When gargoyles fly or if so
did seem
Their vampiric ways are all
a dream
Scary winged creatures, they
fly by night
In dreams of kids, paralyzed
by fright

# GOOD, OLD NOSTALGIA

Nostalgia is life yearning for the past
Yearning for moments it wished would last
The sweet dreams we had to realize
But never endured for all our lives

Brings joy to our hearts, tears to our eyes
Those bittersweet moments back in our lives
Some moments that took our breath away
Oh, how we cherish those every day

And Nostalgia, the place whence they came
Without which life wouldn't be the same
Indulging moments of times past, in future
What then is life without Good, Old Nostalgia

# GOODBYE WINTER WELCOME SPRING

Goodbye Winter Welcome Spring
Hearken! Hear the bluebirds sing
Icy sidewalks dry once more
It's safer then out-of-door
Leafless trees will soon be green
Melted snowbanks wash streets clean
Winter-breaks from school all done
But children never short of fun
Spring-breaks, they're soon to come
With the binge of food and rum
And the moon will re-appear
Signaling that time of year
Longer day and shorter night
Winter's gone out of sight
A blast of pollen in the air
Leaves no doubt that spring is here
Goodbye Winter Welcome Spring
Hearken! Hear the bluebirds sing

# GRANDSON

And here we are, me sitting you
Know this tale, what I went through
For this to happen, for us to meet
For the only job I find so sweet

Over three scores plus two dear friend
Times I thought life's voyage would end
When Life's ups and downs did take hold
Grandma would urge, now you be bold

We pulled up roots back home for here
Where winter's storms are hard to bear
Your dad, our son, he too was fun
Now a man himself and you, his son

His life will have its ups and downs
But you'll be there for smiles, not frowns
Then what's in store for you O friend
Oh, never mind for you're godsend

# HAMMER AWAY

Play the hand you were dealt my son
We had no choice when that was done
This game of life we have to play
You hammer away, just hammer away

The stakes are raised so high my son
You have no choice when that is done
Don't let up for doubt and dismay
So hammer away, just hammer away

# HEARTBREAKING VOODOO GIRL

Far away in the Caribbean sea
many years ago
Appearing in a reverie
smiling all aglow
Her chocolate face in the sun,
her eyes look like pearl
Hair wind-blown and full of fun,
O, Pretty Voodoo Girl
So cute was she and her strange tongue,
He'd to meet that wench
Wouldn't have mattered had it been twang,
she was speaking French
She disappeared in thin air,
to another worl'
Broke his heart, she didn't care
OUCH, Pretty Voodoo Girl

# HIS WIFE AND CHRISTMAS

Her love for dolls and Christmas trees,
he knew it from the start
Now decades old it's plain to see,
she is a young at heart
Her little dolls and pepper lights,
are beautiful to see
And she can't wait till Christmas time,
to decorate the tree

# HOW THEY WANT

To take America back, it seems
Troubling, curious enthymemes
Back from now to whence she came
Back to past and back to same

# HUBRIS

Hubris, O Nemesis, ye punisher of fools
To think they got away with it, to pride or abuse
Pride before destruction, that spirit before the fall
Written in The Proverbs, I tell you one and all
When they fall from grace for it, how naked they look
How wiser to heed those words, written in The Book

# INEVITABILITY

O Man, ye little man, whatever,
will be, will be

Many things, inevitable, beyond
the realm of thee

Ye can't stop a falling star or tame
a raging sea

Death is a certainty and change,
a constant to ye

# IOWANS, HELP US!

Constant beats of their hate drum
Feed our fears, make bigots numb
Once again your turn has come
When we are, you're never mum

With your backs against the wall
Let your voice be heard by all
Sound the death knell, it's your call
Kill those bigots' dream this fall

# IT

How that versatile two-lettered word could be many things we've seen and heard. IT is everything we touch and smell and anything we taste as well. IT could be You, IT could be Me but there are things IT could not be. IT could not be They and not be We, could not be He and not be She. And whenever IT cannot do, remember these four cases of the few.

# IT'S DANCEHALL

It's Dancehall when she's pretty as
a pearl and is a sexiest girl, wants to
rock steady and ska when she's ready,
when she writes a dub poem and she is
willing to show him, when she twerks
and bubble and cause some trouble, if
she has no special move but still loves
the groove, when she would bump and
grind and do the soca wind, when she
loves to rub-a-dub and would do it in
a tub, when she does the hula-hula and
what seems even cooler, when she
dances on pole then gets down and roll,
when she does the belly dance and also
loves to prance, when it's rumba or the
salsa, the samba or the cha-cha and she
wants to rent a tile or just do it any style

# JAMAICAN NOSTALGIA

From far faraway to the northern shore,
they received a frozen dish
To their delight, they couldn't ask for more,
a gift of ackee and fish
And with each bite their minds went back,
went back on the track of time
These moments that those times would lack
when they didn't have a dime
Savoring the taste that was so good
they made an earnest wish
That those friends from faraway would
send some bammy and fish

# JOY

Was her name, a pet name so true
Thought of by wise and good, old uncle, Hugh
Her life shone brightly, two scores plus four
Lit up their lives and they couldn't ask for more

And that little sister, among siblings of six
Wore special boots for one of Nature's tricks
One of her legs was larger than the other
But resilient little Joy, made that no bother

Had a craving for pancake and coffee late at night
Always taking a sibling along, on her fancy's flight
Showed a younger brother how to drink and smoke
And now, looking back, that was a kink and joke

Her favorite 60's music, the good old acid rock
Adored Jimi Hendrix, his stage-craft and shock
And she partied the hardest in her longest dress
Then, in her late teens and passed all those tests

That Nature's trick told the fate she would've met
For it, a symptom was, of what would be her death
And those joyous old memories, they still endure
Lit up their lives and they couldn't ask for more

# KARL AND KIM

(Like Yang and Yin)

She came out of a closet late one
night, then straight into his bed
Still wide awake, to their delight,
this wasn't just in his head

She was the-girl-next-door, to his
surprise too, had a crush on him
And there they were like Yang and
Yin, only the two were Karl and Kim

# KINESTHESIA

Was a girl he knew and
a rare statuesque charm
was she. Was poetry in
motion, mysterious as
the moon and a "men
magnet" said he.
Fingers you like a harp
when she touches you
and her kisses were as
sweet. And he saw her
moves when he shared
her grooves and her
rhythms were a treat.

# LEVITY

When a little boy dreams of flying
Airborne and gravity-defying
Levitating just because he can
Not as a winged creature as a man
Then skirting the stars to touch the moon
And dancing on air to any tune
Rides the wind like a witch on a broom
Rises up like a ghost from a tomb
Perched like a bird on a mountain top
And wishing this dream would never stop

# LIFE'S FLEETING WAYS

Sweet piggyback rides and
bounceabouts, gone too soon
Gone like the wind and like
a popular tune

That all things soon wither
away under the sun
Make hay while the sun
shines, have lots of fun

# LIFE'S TWISTS & TURNS

Life's Twists & Turns they never end
What is, that's next around the bend
And in the grip of doubt and fear
When slow to change, to find that gear
Alas! That's life, the ew, the strange
The twists, the turns, the constant change

# LITLE BIRDIE

Long before thee weighed a pound
She gazed upon her ultrasound
Saw the pea pod and seed within
Her curled up tiny next of kin
A wee raspberry with heartbeat
Named Little Birdie and so sweet

# LOVE

Inebriate with love and what a rye
When that joy of life fills up the heart
They plunged right in, they cast the die
Maybe, pure luck right from the start
Then a fading youth, an empty cage
The ups and downs, love took a hit
All stark reminders of their age
But for forty years, they never quit

# MANDELA AND THE POWER OF ONE

One drop of rain fell in the sea
and a ripple did emerge
Then it grew and grew and grew
and grew until it was a surge
How that surge did multiply into
many a tidal wave
And such was his life on Earth
when he wouldn't become a slave

# MISS ME

Was a powerful phrase that slips
Between that teacup on her lips
Her last wish of grandkids and kids
This old lady was all but wiz

You miss me as I miss my Ma
And miss me as I miss my Pa
Remember me by missing me
And that is all I ask of thee

For a long while she was too stern
But then in time she came to learn
Those grandkids and kids she's got
Are after all, her life and lot

Miss me as I miss my siblings
Miss me as I miss your dribblings
So miss me, miss me, miss me please
That's all I ask of you my kids

# MORE OF WINTER'S IRONIES

For days after that blizzard burst
And those north plains were weathered worst
The snowcapped roofs and snowy lawns
Evade the sun for several dawns

Melting slowly while daydreamers dream
And freezing the nights while lovers steam
Tricky Mother Nature doing her thing
More of Winter's Ironies until spring

# MORTIFIED

To hear bigots speak their fears aloud
Intolerant memes of which they're proud
The xenophobic talk we hear
Is hard to process, hard to bear

Their defending of the status quo
The old tyrannies and so-and-so
The racist meme, their biggest fear
Is hard to process, hard to bear

# MY LOVELY

That wonderful smile My Lovely,
the joy it would impart
Those beautiful eyes My Lovely,
would seize a gazing heart
And how luscious too My Lovely,
vivacious too and smart
You are Nature's gift My Lovely,
right there from the start

# MY MUSE

I took her from a poem
She said she was MY MUSE
Like a genie from a bottle
So I could not refuse
She inspired me with passion
That set my soul afire
And doubled as my genie
Much to my heart's desire

# MY SMILE MAKER

I have seen this rare flower,
one of an exotic seed
Springing up in my garden
and so beautiful indeed
Competing with the daffodils,
my lovely telltale friends
Who dance at the start of spring
to tell me winter ends
Delightful is this flower,
to watch to bloom and grow
Thank You My Smile Maker and
a star of Nature's show

# NATURE'S TRICK

(Telling my little grandson about it)

One winter's day devoid of snow
Sunset played a trick on me
Leafless trees were all aglow
Such wonders still there to see

Darkness descended all about
As the sun crept out of view
Nature's Trick was soon put out
But a miracle did come true

# NOVELTY

What's new may seem better
as the senses perceive
And Novelty like magic, it
so can deceive
Newness is variety, the spice
that we crave
Those perceptions we have
from the cradle to the grave

# NYMPH AND THE BEAST

The horny goddess that she is
To satisfy her carnal needs
Sought and found a ravenous beast
Offered herself for it to feast
So beautiful it found her be
How wonderful a meal would she
The hungry beast soon plays the rake
But still her passions, hard to slake

# O GENTLE KNIGHTS OF YORE

So what of those noble men who
died for chivalry
And who to carry on from them
such meme of gallantry
No knights in shining armors,
more men with hearts of stones
Or did it just die with them and
buried with their bones
O Gentle Knights of Yore, whither
thy spirits went
Whither such valiance be and
whither to be sent
Alas! There's hope, some yearn
for days of ol'
When men would do or die, to
protect each living soul
But whence did those noble men
take gallantry in mind
Chivalry is not dead, it is only
hard to find

# O FATE!

O Fate! How thee chose them to die
In that place, at that time and why?
At the hands of one so evil and dark
One so determined to leave a mark
Of the stain of blood and tears so sad
Their loved ones suffer a loss so bad

And thy master, the devil or God?
Whosoever gave thee the nod
Watched bodies fall to the ground
Round after round after round
And how merciless though art thou
For not telling us who and how

# O WHAT A CHARADE!

Dueling clowns on brinks of cliffs
A dazzling display by twits
They participate as the people wait
In politricks and more antics
Those grifters' grifts and bags of tricks
And what a ruse, they claim a truce
O What a Charade!

# O, SWEET BEL CANTO

What strain of music that we share
The long and luscious notes we hear
That rapid-fire repartee
O, Sweet Bel Canto, night and day

Whence this operatic melody springs
O, Sweet Bel Canto, songs and strings
That haunting music of Puccini
Giordano and Bellini

O, Sweet Bel Canto, from the start
Ye did conquer many a heart
Can soothe a man, can tame a beast
O, Sweet Bel Canto, of thee we feast

# OBLIVION

Somewhere to unload those
things we regret
The graveyard of the mind
for the things we forget

Where bad memories are
interred, the failed ideas too
And all those shattered dreams
that will never come true

# ODE TO A PRAYER WARRIOR

Through thick and thin and sick and sin,
they count on her each day
When times were rough and things got tough,
she fell on her knees to pray
A fearless rock around the clock,
a guardian of the gate
It was her shield and theirs to wield
and so was grandma's faith

# ODE TO A SINNER

And after four scores and plus five
What use it is to be alive
Death toys with him in pangs and pain
Like cat with mouse that writhes in vain
If you love him, they say you do
End this torture, bring him to you
Foil death in death's sadistic ways
He'll join angels to sing thy praise

# ODE TO A WARRIOR'S WIFE

As we set sail into battle
In the spring one early morn
He took a pen and wrote this ode
To his wife who was so torn
After the dirge for winter
By the singing birds of spring
The trees are all leafed again
And O, what a wonderful thing
A sweetened smell of blossoms
Filling the air anew
But I'll miss those winter nights
Cuddling up with you

# ODE TO AMERICA!

Contrite as she will always be
Of any sin or crime
Imperfect as she always was
She stood the test of time
Bad leaders as her people's choice
Is yet another flaw
Determined as she's ever been
To have the rule of law

# ODE TO CHIVALRY

We saw chivalry one night and he was bold
Lifting an old lady, ninety one years old
On his outstretched arms, this gentlest man
Carried her home from a seat in his van
With the ease of giant, it would seem
Carefully, not to disturb her dream
As she slept while on a long, long trip
From family fun and many a sip

# ODE TO THE BACKSTABBERS

We saw it at the Ides of March
when Julius Caesar met his doom
Et tu Brute, he asked a friend,
amongst the stabbers in the room
And then, one by one, they plunged
their knives into Caesar to the last
He said, et tu Brute "and you Brutus"
et tu Brute till he passed
That same thing happened to many
for thousands of years and when
Those they trusted would stab them
in the back, repeatedly and again

# OH, HOW I MISS

Those homegrown gardens in full bloom
With cot or chaise when there is room
Those times of daydreams, reveries
Amidst the flowers and the breeze
Dazzling butterflies everywhere
The sounds of birds are here and there
Oh, How I Miss those clear blue skies
Those moonlit nights that soothe the eyes

# OLD DOG, NEW TRICK

Just when he thinks he's done it all
How life throws him another ball
Once more rising to the occasion
Only now with little persuasion

For now has he's wiser than yore
The old man's a choice to prefer
To babysit grandson not just try
And to sing for him a lullaby

# OLD GLORY (USA)

Old Glory, she is duty-bound,
iron hand in a velvet glove
Helping to keep the peace on
earth, sent from heaven above
She's held up high and mighty
for all the world to see
That hope springs eternally, in
the land of the brave and free

# ON DEATH ROW

Knowing death lingers and that it lurks,
would haunt then in their sleep
The talk of death as death impends,
woud make their flesh do creep
They'd wish death come and go so fast,
with little time to weep
In a fateful rendezvous with death,
they pray their soul to keep

# ON THE CATWALK

She's poetry in motion, a
beautiful work of art
A flawless creation, perfected
from the start
A possessor of unmatched
elegance and style
Rivaling Mona Lisa, flashing
that smile

# ON TYRANTS (Castro etc)

Even the devil has admirers
Then why are we perplexed
That evil men of one generation
Are heroes to the next

# OUT OF THE MOUTHS OF BABES

Out of The Mouths of Babes
and Sucklings came
Those words of wisdom just
the same
Then with the heart and mind
of one so young
Whence came this knowledge
from thy tongue
And with each generation that
has passed
The young would then learn
twice as fast
And demonstrably so since
Man evolved
Yet another mystery still
unsolved

# POLICE BRUTALITY

Armed with badges and guns of State
Some use their guns as tools of hate
So on their own these rogues in blue
Choose their subjects based on hue
Bang, bang, bang, another one dies
Out in the street, they fall like flies
Not mourned by all like heroes are
They're victims of an insidious war
As their loved ones writhe in distress
Their names are savaged in the Press
That Blacklivesmatter, out in the street!
Until there's justice, never retreat!

# PRETTY GIRLS

Shed winter's covers by late spring,
then some more by summer
Such a treat to see them swing, in all
their glitz and glamour
Boys and men are now agaze like
mimics of birdwatchers
Fawned at, flattered as always, Pretty
Girls are eye-catchers
Savor these moments in the sun, for
soon it will be fall
Then winter's covers end the fun for
Pretty Girls, short and tall

# REQUIEM FOR A DESPOT

Brave eagle soared across the sky
Raised Old Glory, did she fly
On battleships out in the blue
Fully briefed on what to do

They sent a shot across the bows
To despots all and freedom's foes
For good did triumph over bad
When good men stood up to Assad

# REVOLUTION

Clip by clip, chip by chip,
a despot loses grip
Drip by drip, slip by slip,
This tyrant bound to trip

# SAY GOODBYE TO THUNDERSTORMS

Summer time was here again, the
time of year we hike
Those dog days couldn't end too
soon for time again to bike

When riding on this summer's eve
there was a summer breeze
Tickled our noses like butterflies
until it made us sneeze

And then it whispered in our ears
something nice and sweet
Say Goodbye To Thunderstorms and
sweltering summer heat

# SEX

What a greater power art thou, the cause of many sins
That maketh whores of some women and sinners of some saints
Cause many a kingdom to end in ruins and marriage in divorce
When great men falter, fall from grace ye art usually the source
That some men are consumed by thee, art ye nature's gift or curse
As to lovers' hearts put asunder, there's nothing that is worse

# SHE, HIS NEMESIS

One by one at the primary stage
He slew sixteen when battles rage
Triumphantly, he sealed his fate
A final battle, it did await
Inside the theater was a last foe
For the final battle of that row
She, His Nemesis, was there to toil
To end his run and to cause his foil

# SHINGLES

Fireflies dancing in the dark
Spiders crawling on the wall
In her optical illusion
Their babies stumble and fall

Now in this winter of her life
Numbering four scores and six
In all her pain and confusion
Her eyes play all these tricks

And after thirty days in bed
Visible signs are all gone
Only this is no conclusion
As the pain still lingers on

When on one side of her body
It itches, burns and tingles
It was never a delusion
That grandma got the Shingles

# SHREDDED SOME OLD MEMORIES

Shredded some Old Memories,
Put them in the trash
Not to recycle
To turn them into ash
Buried in old poems
Written long ago
Had to make new ones
And wrote a book to show

# SLAVES OF TYRANNY

May bombs of freedom find
their mark
Free Slaves of Tyranny from
the dark
And may the winds of change
sweep those lands
Free them from the grip of the
tyrants' hands

# SO MUCH MORE TO DEVOUR

There is so much more to learn,
we shudder to explore
The depths of our ignorance,
we'd rather be unsure
So Much More To Devour
all these years after school
Better to die not knowing
than to prove yourself a fool

# SONNET OF A STRONGER LOVE

Drunk with love that intoxicant
Now his hold on her was all gone
And begging her soon turned to rant
No longer his prize possession

And why did it seem so unfair
To see his pride just walk away
A jilted lover, that was clear
From anything he had to say

Now the tables were turned on him
Her heart was now happy and free
She's found a stronger love with Tim
Too late for him on bended knee

Then he turned his eyes up to the sky
And kept asking her why, why, why

# SONNET OF ANOTHER DAY

Amidst the gloom and the doom
Kids frolic on a sunny day
And what attention they consume
What joy it is to watch them play

Then sunset followed by twilight
A moonlit night and starry skies
And we rise again by daylight
To singing birds and butterflies

Those dark clouds that bring us rain
Among the reasons that we pray
Their silver linings not as plain
But thank Thee for Another Day

Amidst the gloom and the doom
And what attention they consume

# SONNET OF BEAUTY AND THE WILD

Early one morn, one summer day, she
went streaking in the wood
At times her passions are unchained and
that's never understood

They could feel her passions in the wind
and nothing could stay still
And it seems the woods groove with her
as she shares with it, her thrill

So surreal a thing to see, when beauty
meets the wild
All creatures, great and small alike,
protect her as their child

Then in the wood, misunderstood,
a beautiful child of the wild

# SONNET OF COLD SWASHBUCKLER

Cold Swashbuckler, he tells them the tales
One hook-hand and a sword in the next
What secrets there are of the seas he sails
The old scalawag is ruthless at best

He says he's the only pirate there is
Plunder of pillage earned him that spot
To rule the lanes of the seven seas
With just one eye, the other was shot

Never enough is the pillage in hand
He'd put crew men to walk the planks
And he raids villages further inland
For mistakenly seizing ships with blanks

Aye, aye Swashbuckler left horrors of trails
A wicked old pirate telling his tales

# SONNET OF COME AWAY WITH ME

Come away with me O frien'
On this trip down memory lane
Take a joy ride way back when
Where life was all but inane

Come away with me O frien'
Thank small mercies as we should
Live those moments once again
Not the bad ones only good

Come away with me O frien'
To recount what did befall
Take a notebook and a pen
So much there to recall

Come away with me O frien'
Take a joy ride way back when

# SONNET OF HEARTBREAK, THAT SILENT KILLER

Greatest nemesis of Cupid yet
Be them weak, be them strong
Sends countless lovers to their death
For choosing others who were wrong

This silent killing that you do
Be them coward, be them brave
That punish lovers who are true
Insidiously send them to their grave

Yet not all the time that you succeed
Some star-crossed lovers are no longer
Not all would succumb to your deed
The irony, you made them stronger

Be them saddened, be them blue
Would have nothing to do with you

# SONNET OF HOODIE, THY SON

Police sent him walking
After you were shot dead
With a line he's talking
In self-defense, they said
Said you went for his gun
Or if so he did warn
But how could that son
Only if it was drawn

And what did he intend
Since Hoodie can't talk
That you had to defend
This killer may walk

But slowly O, little man
Justice, she's just began

# SONNET OF O, DARK DAY AT THE TOWER

First, they were four
Then they were eight
It took four more
Before it was straight

How oft that seating
Changed by the hour
For that secret meeting
That day at the tower

The gift was the Kremlin's
To three of the shady
Of a thousand gremlins
For The Teflon Lady

That dark day at the tower
Of hostile foreign power

# SONNET OF ONLY TIME WILL TELL

And whither those days and years are gone
Looking in the mirror, trying to see
Those ticks we hear is time marching on
Leaving us behind on life's journey

Those lifelines tell a tale or two
What secrets they hold of what shall be
Time took a toll but you're still you
Only time will tell. it is the key

One of the things that we know for sure
We're here today and gone tomorrow
There is the time when we're no more
Leaving behind some pain and sorrow

Those ticks we hear is time marching on
And whither those days and years are gone

# SONNET OF SANTANA

(Mozart of his music)

This Maestro of the Latin beat
His guitar melodies sweet as wine
In music theaters, on the street
The other parts are just as fine

Black Magic Woman, what a treat
We dance and sing it line by line
That song, Smooth, is just as sweet
We'd still be rocking as we dine

His Latin tempo packed with heat
With all the Pieces so divine
Would keep a full room on its feet
Santana's music, always mine

And he plays the music O, so sweet
This Maestro of the Latin beat

# SONNET OF SPIRIT OF OLD GLORY

Behold the eagle spreads its wings
Hearken, hear O trumpets call!
It urgently soars with the winds
What now, what next, to befall

Cowards flinch, they shirk to fight
None on a ship or on the shore
Brave men ready with all their might
Such love of country can't be more

For in the balance, freedom hangs
That, they sacrificed to defend
Our hopes and dreams, still in hands
When those battles came to an end

And Spirit of Old Glory was revealed
By brave men in heaven, on that field

# SONNET OF THE BLACK STALLION

Unbroken black stallion, equine beast
O, savoring your moment in the sun
Cantering gracefully towards the east
Streaming tail and mane as you run

Beautiful creature of nature you are
Seemingly, putting that charm on display
One of the most powerful ones by far
Mesmerizing watchers of you all day

Dallying boastfully with that white mare
How wonderful to see, you are no dud
Prancing, dancing she neighs as you rear
Oh shinny black stallion, you are a stud

They gallop away in the wind so free
How picturesque a sight for us to see

# SONNET OF THE BLUEBIRDS

To hear the bluebird woos the hen
From the grassland across the blue
Melodies sweet, we counted ten
On to the nest site flew the two

To see the bluebird woos the hen
And never stopped until she cooed
Flapped his wings again and again
How soon to welcome a new brood

To watch four bluebirds as they fly
On to the grassland where they fed
From the nest site towards the sky
Then back to nest where they bed

To hear the bluebird woos the hen
Melodies sweet, we counted ten

# SONNET OF THE DARING, DAMNED DEVIL

Out on the boardwalk late one night
When suddenly, right out of the blue
That moonlit ocean was a great sight
What wasn't a dream, did come true

Appearing out there right before the eyes
All dressed in spike heels and a short dress
Was the daring, damned devil in disguise
She whispered in the dark, "Hi, I'm Tess"

Her warm embrace, it had extra heat
So unreal and there was no way to tell
And her sweet kiss, it was extra sweet
How she was the devil straight from hell

Daring, damned devil disguised, down towns
Up from the dark deep doing the rounds

# SONNET OF THE DECIDER

This cross that is to bear is hard
Then why must it be done at all
Must tell them like it is O Lord
And someone has to make the call

Not everyone can face the truth
That all of it can then be told
At times it can be like a brute
To face it down one must be bold

It may be tough, it may be bad
But whatever there is to tell
Possibly cold and maybe sad
Do it fairly and do it well

This cross that is to bear is hard
Must tell them like it is O Lord

# SONNET OF THE ELEMENTS

Sun did not come out to play
Night conspired to make it so
When snow had stolen the day
By covering that sunny glow

Daybreak brings new game in town
Old sun decides it had enough
Vengeful rays now streaming down
A friendly wind would lend a puff

Blows those vapors to whence they came
But not for long upon the plains
Ends this bout of a snowy game
Where they'd return as heavy rains

And lucky are those, to see this bout
Than suffer the consequence of drought

# SONNET OF THE GREAT BEYOND

She bites the bullet, faces her fears
The least of which, is that she dies
Now in the twilight of her years
Then in the beyond, what there lies

Breathed her first, her life-clock ticks
Took life's journey, had a great past
She'd long ago, four scores and six
Now here she is, to breathe her last

No way to tell what will occur
She prays the Lord her soul to save
But what's in store ahead for her
There in heaven beyond the grave

And how to tell, who to respond
Out there from, the great beyond

# SONNET OF THE NOW

Nothing will last
None of the fun
What's passed is past
Under the sun

Even the hate
And the love too
Will dissipate
All that is true

Cherish the now
Just to be clear
No matter how
Always be fair

Try to do good
All of us should

# SONNET OF THE RENAISSANCE

We see the years come and go
See the twilight then the dawn
That yesterday was tomorrow
Out of darkness comes the morn

The phoenix rises from the dirt
The sunset ushers in the night
From its ashes to rebirth
Then the sunrise, the daylight

Then we're gone as those that fell
And life continues the rebirth
Gone to heaven and gone to hell
The Renaissance right here on earth

We see the years come and go
That yesterday was tomorrow

# SONNET OF THE SCARY NIGHT OF A 7-YEAR-OLD

He watches the fireflies roam the dark
Pulls the pillow over his head
Cringes when the hound dogs growl and bark
As monsters march around his bed

He dreams of flying like a dove
They chase him soaring through the air
Into a flight of hawks above
He jumps up shivering from the fear

Soon he would fall asleep once more
But when it was time for him to rise
And now with the lights on for sure
Taking his time to open eyes

And when he'd fall asleep once more
He did with the lights on for sure

# SONNET OF THE TEMPEST & THE CREW

The tempest swept across the blue
Those men stuck to charted course
Tossed that ship, would test its crew
They set the sails against her force

They went below into the hull
Fixed as much time would allow
Then back on deck into the lull
To fix the stern and fix the bow

Stuck to charted course once more
The tempest's tail did soon appear
Prayed that ship not wash ashore
Those bold men did not despair

And when the tempest was all done
That ship and crew welcomed the sun

# SONNET OF THE "TINSEL HAIR" OGRE

The Ogre, cornered in the town
None more deadlier than that beast
Now he's sensing, going down
Time to end this hate-filled feast

For months some entertained that brute
Who's just a beast, never a man
Then slowly he would learn the truth
Devoid of wit to fill their plan

Now face to face, a potent foe
He sees no future in her eyes
A cornered beast, nowhere to go
She executed his demise

And what was there for kids to learn
The Ogre's way is slash and burn

# SONNET OF THIS IS HELL

For all its gloom, all its doom
Watch the news or read a blog
There's no hell beyond the tomb
See what's lurking in the fog

Pangs of hell and much ado
Lie in bed afraid to sleep
Evil's eyes are watching you
All those nightmares of the deep

Futile are the fleeting bliss
Goddamn devil doth deceive
One way out of this abyss
Pray to God for his reprieve

Mark my ode for what it's worth
This is hell right here on earth

# STEATOPYGIA

A female form that we sight,
what is a "rear" beauty
An aberration of delight,
they call the big booty

This African gene is all right
for women of a type
For even yellow, even white,
big booty is the hype

# STIMMING ON LIFE

Day time and night time we stim away
On repetitive routines day by day
Those calls of nature, we would do
But the rest is up to me and you
We stim to escape the stress and strife
Or do it to enjoy some things in life
Yet Stimming On Life is not a choice
Like choosing a virtue over vice
And when we no longer stim on that wave
It is when we are six feet in the grave

# TEARS OF JOY

I saw me a paradox but one that's
borne of love
A tale of joy and sadness straight
from heaven above

She cries those Tears of Joy every
time her baby cries
And when they have to separate
each time of her goodbyes

A gift of love to lovers, an
overwhelming joy
Their cutest little baby girl or
cutest little boy

# THAT FOREVER THING

O, what a trouble is that thing
Can't not miss it in a fling
You don't see it in the eyes
And can hear it in goodbyes
Some may taste it in a meal
Others seal it in a deal
One may sense it's not to be
Could be difficult to see
When it seems it will not last
Try to leave it in the past

# THAT OLE CHIVALRY, THE REUNION

(Inspired by my friend, Craig A Davis, a Vet)

Then once again, their paths were crossed
Two Knights, a quest for chivalry, lost
Now older and wiser with much to share
Their search for chivalry, too much to bear
The battle-scarred Knight would tell his tale
Of how close it came, his health to fail
And his friend who had no scars to show
Happy to see him but sad to know
Of That Ole Chivalry, their search would rest
On knowing their sons continue the quest

# THAT PASSION

That Passion gave us love galore
The hearts and souls of much amore
Love of mankind, love of friends
Love of family and a fourth depends

On the love of lovers that we share
For the love of lovers that we care
That love is Eros, all four are great
And yet some still find room for hate

# THAT TASTE OF STRAWBERRIES

He sees her strawberries upon the mound
And relishes it when fantasies abound
One of those fantasies, there in his mouth
That Taste of Strawberries, her without doubt

# THE BATTLE OF PTSD

After the battles, after the war
Away from the battlefield, far, far, far
One last battle before they die
O, brave warriors could make you cry

Battling the demons that they see
Invisible enemies to you and me
A final battle yet to be won
After all they did, after all was done

# THE BEAR AND THE EAGLE

Shadows of The Bear and The Eagle loom
With freedom's rise and old tyrannies' doom
And so The Bear stumbles, the tyrannies fall
While The Eagle soars to the people's call
As to their tug of war, now decades old
But such a history there to be told

# THE BEGGARS

Early to rise he would hit the streets
He gives an howdy to those he meets
Engages them in topics they'd like
And that beggar, he even owns a bike

But long, long ago when I was young
The Beggars I saw, they didn't have tongue
With a outstretched hand they came to you
That look in their eyes said what to do

How times might change a beggar's fate
Now he can even be a ward of State
The Beggars today, they're ready to choose
What to accept and what to refuse

# THE BOGEYWOMAN

(To be read in your Vincent Price" voice)


I have this tale, a tale to tell
So listen up and listen well
It started when she was a wench
Her hopes and dreams were for the bench
But soon a pol would change her life
And then with that would come the strife
She'd be a pol and run, she did
A thousand gremlins plagued her bid
Spawned by reds to help her foe
After her loss she had to go
So gone she was to disappear
leaving in her wake, this nightmare
She's in their dreams and in their beds
In their thoughts and in their heads
The Bogey Woman, it must be said
Would never go till they are dead

(Then Google the "Vincent Price" laughter)

# THE BRINKMEN

To send a message to the Korean Turds
This leader did not mince his words
No more threats to my people, he said
Or fire and fury shall kill you dead

As the world looked on in shock and awe
There're woes and sighs and cries of nah
From the land of the free to lands afar
No one wanted a nuclear war

# THE CYCLE OF LIFE

They trip they tumble the toddlers play
In between catnaps they do that all day
Feed them on time and we clean them too
And instead of a cry we hope they coo

An exercise in behavior control
And this labor of love could take a toll
But to bear the pain is never in vain
The Cycle of Life is hard to maintain

# THE DAUNTLESS

Living our lives on freedom street
where The Dauntless conquered
tyranny
The Dauntless dared to take the heat
so we live their dream of destiny
Living our lives on freedom street
where The Dauntless conquered
tyranny
Those Founders battled hard to beat
the masters of a colony

# THE DIVE OF THE COUNTDOWN

Hear O, a symphony
deep beneath the blue
And strangely, the dream
that it would imbue

Miles from the ocean,
sleeping in a town
And dreaming of The Dive
of The Countdown

Shylock with Beethoven

To see the dream. search
for it at:
http://youtu.be/tC48nKm-law

# THE EROTIC LOVE

How passionate art thou from the heart
Still hard to tell ye and lust apart
But when thou art true ye would endure
Then and only then we can be sure
That thou art The Erotic Love
And came from heaven above
Yet ye do make lunatics of some
Some fools smarter and wise ones dumb
Making some cry from a broken heart
But doing countless wonders from the start

# THE FALLING TEAR DROP

The servant of darkness,
he came for you
When your guard was down
and you posed no threat
With a gun and a badge,
disguised in blue
That guardian angel was
an angel of death
And The Falling Tear Drop
never stops
While servants of darkness
do what they do
Let our guardian angels
be good cops
O Father in heaven let
them be true

# THE FEMINIST

He saw his mother through the years
Bit the bullet and calmed her fears
For what to come with grace and wit
She met each task with guts and grit
His father was a Policeman
How mother too would work and plan
For both to him had equal roles
They shared the joy and too the woes
These values were with him for good
But now a man, he understood
That equal rights, they did exist
And why he was, The Feminist

# THE GLORIFIED DRAG QUEEN

Female Illusionist, he calls herself
For now, The Transvestite, is moot
This Fairy, Drag Queen, now calls himself
Female Illusionist, to boot

# THE GREAT ESCAPE

Then trapped beneath the ocean floor
The remains of many a Dinosaur
Over time would escape in oil galore
Via man-made rigs from sea to shore

# THE GREATEST STILL

He would float like a butterfly
and sting like a bee
He is The Greatest, aka,
Muhammad Ali
While dancing on air and
pedaling on his toes
This brilliant pugilist would
vanquish his foes
Rhyming like a poet and
stepping up the pace
He would floor an opponent
with those fists with grace
And now that he is gone
from those bouts of skill
How we savor the moments
of The Greatest Still

# THE HETEROSEXUAL BOY

I like girls, he said, I like girls,
from the time I could see
The little pearls with curls,
they are beautiful to me

And I like boys, I like boys too
but not in that way
For they are not as beautiful
and that's all I will say

# THE JOY OF WORDS

(Inspired by my grandson)

There is this lad who loves to read
The Joy of Words, soon fill his heart
He just turned three, just three, indeed
But he did have an early start

For long before he was three
I read to him rhythms and rhymes
While he was sitting on my knee
Not just once but many times

# THE LITTLE SUN CATCHER

Her sun-drop pendants all stood still
Hanging above her windowsill
Icicle droplets all hand-blown
Attached to a string, pointing down

Up from the mountain come the fun
To see those pendants catch the sun
Her little prisms would cast so bright
All around her room, a rainbow light

# THE LONE WOLVES

Hearken some advice my friends
and herein lies a twist
Stop whistling pass the graveyard,
there're lone wolves in our midst
If we see them build an arsenal,
that should be of concern
How many of us would have to die,
before we have to learn
That born with the right to bear arms,
such shooters are awry
Now stop the partisan bicker
and try to find out why

# THE MILKY WAY

Once upon The Milky Way
I saw the strangest thing
Many miles from heaven's gate
The angels came to sing

Beautiful, the sweet refrain
My heart was overjoyed
Then to find this but a dream
Awakened and Annoyed

Sinners can get to heaven
Just not the way of dreams
Once upon The Milky Way
You're on the way it seems

# THE OLD LADY & THE GRIM REAPER

For years she lives up in the attic
And what she isn't, is erratic
Tumbling down the stairs one night
End over end, flight after flight
The landing she had was hard as rock
Leaving her household in horror and shock
Grim Reaper took her while she dreamed
He came too soon, too soon, it seemed
For now awakened from her sleep
She has no memory of the creep

# THE OLD LADY UPSTAIRS

Survived a fall down a stairwell
Now this strange tale that she'd tell
Said, when at nights, she has to go
To pass that stairwell to and fro
That creepy stairwell that she fears
Is like an abyss, not the stairs

# THE OLD MAN

A few times, afraid
and sometimes real bold
He tells us those tales
but kept others untold
Where dreams are memories
and memories were dreams
That's what matters to
The Old Man, it seems
And now he's lost in
reverie
Happy is he, for he
hums like a bee

# THE PAUPER & THE POET

Our fates forbid that we should switch
But I need your help to make me rich
Give me words of thundering sounds
Words with sway that have no bounds
Words of wisdom and the truth
Words to share those with the youth
I'm just a pauper wanting to learn
Can't give thee anything in return
Except to thank thee for this deed
This gift of gab was all I need

# THE PREACHER

Though the "Rod and Bible wielding"
ways of this man
Scare the living hell out of each and
everyone
They flock whither he went, to tents
that they pitch
Giving him millions in tithes and
making him rich
And he waxes the scripture while
waving that Rod
Then asserts, he is wielding the right
hand of God

# THE REBELS

Rolled the dice and what a price
That all that blood would spill
For their right they had to fight
Thank God they had the will
Here they band with guns in hand
Still wary of a ruse
Man to man no battle plan
To sit and talk a truce

# THE RISE OF THE TEFLON LADY

Old patriarchs tried to stop her rise
But The Teflon Lady was too wise
So now they have to deal with this
They've got their knickers in a twis'
For thirty years those troglodytes
Did fail to violate her rights
And those of hubby who was prez
With vast Right-wing conspiracies
Now there she was, a threat to them
Those desperate men now at the helm
We don't expect they would admit
She thwarted them with grace and grit

# THE SORCERESS

By the sleight of hand
without a flaw
She magically bends
Mother Nature's law

Disappearing acts seem
more than trick
She dazzles the crowd
with black magic

When unsuspectingly
they'd cheer
Some folks did vanish
in thin air

Her creepy deed though,
did not last
They soon awoke from
the spell she cast

# THE SUN vs. THE WIND

Touched by The Sun this morning
It did get her out of bed
Enjoy the thrill of summer still
More heat to come, it said

Kissed by The Wind this morning
And it whispered in her ear
This summer heat will soon retreat
My autumn does draw near

# THE SURVIVOR

With roving eyes, a staggering gait and not
knowing where he be

Cursing shadows and yelling at the wind,
what manner of man is he

And he battles demons, night and day,
a fight that's hard to see.

But in the end 'twas him alone, for the long
haul, still him alone, triumphantly, his will
alone, that made that man be free

# THE TEFLON LADY & THE "TINSEL HAIR" OGRE

The Teflon Lady was wooing the town
When The "Tinsel Hair' Ogre hunts her down
Towering, snorting and pacing around
Uttering that incoherent, rambling sound
And she handled that monster with grace and grit
After she learned he was just a twit

# THE THUG

He was but a lad until his death,
then soon was called The Thug
Entangled in the crackers' net,
they slew him with a slug

That lad unarmed, never a threat,
somehow became a bug
To crackers who took his breath,
and did it with a shrug

# THE WAY YOU SMILE

(Bart to Trish)

Wicked 'n' wil', The Way You Smile,
how much I love those lips
It took a while though not my style,
for me to come to grips
With finding out without a doubt,
I am in love with thee
I love your mouth, that wicked pout,
now plant a kiss on me

# THEIR TRIAD TRYST

A tale of two, no three lovers and one
was but a guy
That erotic fest in their love nest and he,
a little shy
Touchy-feely, sexy, needy, hers could
be the case
Passions push her to possess a craving
for such a taste
That lesbian lust and love she must was
never refused
Their Triad Tryst was never missed and
he was so amused

# THEN OVER IN DAMASCUS

Women mowed down by tanks,
in streets now covered with stains
Furious men then took up arms
across Mideastern plains

They joined in with the rebels and
used jihad as tool
Battling him night and day, to end
the tyrant's rule

And the world kept wondering
about a war from hell
Was this jihad of chivalry, only
time would tell

# THEN OVER IN MOSCOW

Old Mother Kremlin, she's in a dream
Of a glorious, old, Cold-Warring scheme

She then set out to have annexed
Even with the whole world so vexed

Parts of the empire she once grew
Her old ambitions tried anew

And to awake this rogue with the nukes
Would soon require more than rebukes

# THERE'RE SOULS IN LIMBO

And angels warn, there'll
be much to regret
A life unprepared has to
choose beyond death
There're Souls In Limbo
with no way to tell
Which way to heaven, and
which way to hell
A choosing of theirs and
for them to do
When words go unheeded,
when angels imbue

# THINGS WE BUILT

Things We Built and left behind,
they were really life's portals
Earthly gateways left in time,
for use by other mortals

And after all been said and done,
each was just a slave
Shackled to an ordered estate,
right down to the grave

# THIS APPLE MADNESS

And silently they finger-tap
The tiny screens they use to snap
They dance to beats that you can't hear
From Apple gadgets everywhere
The addicts of this handheld screen
Some talk on phones that are not seen
'twas one man's passion to invent
This Apple Madness, evident
Yet so much good that is can do
But here, too many to go through

# THIS CYCLE OF HATE

And when men's souls are ripped away
There's nothing left of them but clay
Without their souls they have no faith
Their empty vessels then fill with hate
Faithless and hateful now are they
They rip the souls of men away

And when men's soul are ripped away

# THIS TEMPLE

I saw me a temple and I wonder
whence it came
There were other temples but this
one, not the same
I got me some pictures to take
a closer look
And found me this work of art
and the mastery it took

God took some clay and molded it
into the perfect form
Gave it a mind, a soul and a heart
that was warm
And now exists This Temple
as beautiful as can be
He must have broken that mold for
it's the only one I see

# THOSE FEET

Those feet would take you anywhere
With all the weight they had to bear
Those early steps from crib to floor
Would turn to years of countless more
They'd only rest when you would do
Would only rise when you would too
Such loyalty and duty-bound
Those feet were first to hit the ground
And when life's journey had to end
Those feet were really your best friend

# THOSE GLORY DAYS

Those Glory Days are gone old frien'
And never to be seen again
You did good deeds and what a price
Your selflessness and sacrifice
These virtues are their own reward
Honoring you in that regard

# THOSE GOD-PLAYERS

Doers and ushers at the gateway of life
Practiced in a stethoscope and in a knife
Mimicking Mother Nature on their rounds
But Those God-players, they are no clowns

They heal the sick and wrestle with death
Sometimes they lose and win that bet
When babies cry in their arms at birth
Mothers are assured, for what it's worth

For most, they do this by their faith
And some, a choice or family trait
For what is done, say thanks, you should
Those God-players, so smart, so good

# THOSE HANDS I TRUST

Two roads to travel,
which one I might
One leads to darkness,
one leads to light
Two roads to travel,
which one I should
One leads to evil,
one leads to good
Two roads to travel,
which one to take
Must choose the right
one, too much at stake
Two roads to travel,
choose one I must
Put it in God's hands,
Those Hands I Trust

# THOSE LIFELINES

Those lifelines tell a tale or two
How long a life, how long ado
The crow's feet are a sign of age
A wrinkled neck, the look of sage
Long time passed the prime of life
Wiser from the throes of strife
So Those Lifelines, they truly tell
For what it's worth, they do bode well

# THOSE SACRED OATHS

Those Sacred Oaths that men would take
There're times when men must take a stand
Ever bound by them for goodness sake
Those times a man must show his hand
When conscience guides a wavering mind
And good men know it, that they must
To cast that selfishness behind
Or break Those Sacred Oaths we trust

# THOSE TINY TOTS

Those Tiny Tots those tantrums throw
But only because to let us know
The sooner they learn to talk and write
The sooner to end those tantrums' plight

# THOSE TRUMPETERS

Of those discordant sounds they blare
So jarring to the ears
Many a dream turns to nightmare
When playing up the fears
Please let us hear their silence and
It cannot be too late
For Those Trumpeters blow louder
When playing up the hate

# TIME OF HALLOWEEN

Two "apple head" witches
stirring up a stew
A "pumpkin head' demon
watches as they do

Their steamy green broth
of Halloween slime
Signals once again, soon
Halloween time

Add a "bug head, spider
leg and bat wing" brew
Clearly that's a meal for
more than the two

Then when a thousand
brooms came swooping in
You could tell it was a
Time of Halloween

And wolves howled as their
mouths watered with thirst
But they stayed well away
till the witches dispersed

# TINGLE WITH LOVE

O Tess, a romantic as
romantic could be
Bart took her for granted,
how foolish was he
Her shrew did show him
the wrath of her tongue
What was almost a fling
was then all flung
Then he sent her a note
of empathy
That he hoped would
reverse her apathy
To his pleasant surprise
she did accede
And now the two Tingle
With Love, indeed

# 'TIS NATURE'S FAULT

Illicit love and whence
it came
Two hearts like magnets,
two souls entwine
One love, one heart is
not a game
When two loves were
lost but found in time
Two lives now changed,
never the same
'tis Nature's Fault and
not a crime

# TO THE ARABS FIGHTING FOR FREEDOM

Fight, fight, fight, with all your might, 300 years to freedom is never too late! Fight, fight, fight, for you are right, that freedom is possible when you keep the faith!

# TODDLER

Your first six steps of the joy and strife
Toddling for days on the tracks of life
Valleys are deep and mountains to climb
On a long trip on a journey through time
With more ups and downs in life to be
Still there're many a wonder to see
Places to go and people to meet
A lot depends on those two feet
Walk on little one, finish the deed
A bon voyage to you, and Godspeed

# TRAGEDY OF THE HEARTS

Spurned by her who
was true at the start
Star-crossed lovers
for many years
A cuckold, blue, died
a broken Heart
And when she heard
she shed no tears

# TWICE THE MAN

(Inspired by my son)

How best to measure a man,
if not by his kin
By his promise to make his son
Twice The Man of him
Those words are cast in concrete
by him, so he pledged
He'll make those words his deeds
so that promise won't be wedged
And what manner of man who
would swear so to do
For such a man has got to be
twice a man he knew

# TWO KNIGHTS AND OL' CHIVALRY

(Inspired by my friend, Craig A. Davis, a Vet)

Two Knights, a quest, what truth to seek
Will the strong still protect the weak
Much gallantry, they found, shore to shore
Ol' Chivalry Lives! The quest, no more
And those two Knights, put to a test
Found Ol' Chivalry and end a quest
One, a hero from long ago
The other, he had no scars to show
They became friends, joined at the heart
Then it was time for them to part
Our paths will cross again O friend
Maybe not soon but in the end

# TYPOLAND

Tick, tick, tick, tick, tock, tock, tock
Keyboards working around the clock
Fingers and thoughts are out of sync
Maybe we're going too fast to think
And we still can't seem to understand
Ending up there in Typoland
Words misspelled and Freudian slips
No time to see annoying blips
Tick, tick, tick, tick, tock, tock, tock
Keyboards working around the clock
Fingers………..

# UNREQUITED LOVE, NO LONGER (Bart to Tess)

Flights of fancy, visions of thee
Lustful dreams and reverie
Burning desire deep inside
For thirteen years it did abide
An aching mind, a depressed soul
A broken heart, all took toll

But now I thank thee to requite
For I love thee with all my might
We suffer so that love could live
A noble cause to which we give
And that chivalry did affect our lives
What luck too! This love survives

# UNTIL SHE MET OLD NICK

How dutiful, how unfulfilled,
a wife she would be
Until She Met Old Nick and
is promised to be free
And whence came this succubus
that took possession of her
From the dark side whither she
went, in the dark days of yore
Now exorcized, she seeks to tell
the tales so very well
Of her exploits in the dreams
of men, as a creature from hell

# UNTIL YOU MET HER SHREW

Mark my words young man for this
you never knew
You'll never know this scorn of hers,
unless you meet her shrew
Now you reminisce how she you miss
and regret those things you'd do
But you never knew this scorn of hers,
Until You Met Her Shrew

# WARNING!

Nothing is ever what is seems to be
In a world of sinners and trickery
When down is up and up is down
That every smile could be a frown
Girls in pants and guys in drags
Can't tell the difference by the tags
A heterosexual could be gay
If he's bisexual in the hay
Where politicians lips would lie
Then kiss the babies, make them cry
We hear the words some preachers preach
And they should practice what they teach
When bad is good and good is bad
How to tell then, what is fad
Some merchants sell us things online
Then share our data free of fine
And children can't tell right from wrong
Taking cues from a sinner's song
What's more to say about this news
But to warn you on how you choose

# WATCH US BANTER

When that evil would lurk in broad daylight
Away from the shadows and the dark of night
The sight of his daughter defiled and slain
Her father would wince in anger and pain
Neighbors are shocked and they empathized
A nation sighed but desensitized
As life moves on to another day
Watch Us Banter and watch us play

# WAVES

They ebb and flow, they come and go
And vanish away just like the snow
Fleeting as the winds when they race
Then disappear without a trace
And before long they reappear
But how to tell just when and where
Changing momentum and their trend
Those short-lived waves will soon end

# WE SEE YOU

We See You through that manmade lens
inside your mother's womb
That place from where you would commence
your voyage onto the tomb

Two temples where it's dark and dense
where life would start and end
Whither you are bound, when and whence,
you're never alone O friend

# WEDDED

Then, him and her
No my, no your
They did agree
As she and he

Not I but we
Be us, not me
Not mine, not yours
Or his and hers

Now, you and I
To do or die
Our at ours
Tango and showers

Through thick and thin
We will, we win
One love, one heart
Till death, do us part

# WHAT A FOOL

When a man ignores
a good advice
He's now then left to
his own device
What A Fool he'd be
to shun the wise
When that could mean
his own demise

# WHAT BETTER WAY TO DIE

Why fight then if not to win
the battles that we must
On land, sea, in hidden caves
and in the desert dust
What Better Way To Die than
to save God-given rights
For when we fail our children
will have to fight our fights

# WHAT DID SHE SEE IN ME?

She said, each is one but two are we.
What did ye see in me?
Then for forty years we would be
together
Weathering the storms like birds of
a feather
And now we are one and one are we.
What Did She See In Me?

# WHAT MANNER OF MEN

What Manner of Men, not hard to infer
Cravens and cowards are wont to differ

To no avail, they sit to confer
And when they cower then not to deter

The deeds of tyrants are bound to recur
With hundreds of thousands more to inter

# WHAT WOULD HAVE BEEN, IF HE HAD?

Worked much harder when in school
Not been one to play the fool
Married a different girl he kissed
Seized the chances that he missed
Become the artist he could be
Painted what his mind did see
Been more punctual for his work
Not been sometimes such a jerk
Had a desire to be rich
Just been a little more selfish
Given more love when he should
Done more good when he could
Worshipped God and had more faith
Practiced patience, learned to wait
Taken more chances in his life
Shown more confidence in his wife
Another chance to be that dad
What Would Have Been, If he had?

# WHEN DEMONS ZOOM

And When Demons Zoom in from their
tomb in search of hopeless souls
They pick the sick and the addict and
the weak to fill their goals

They hover around and they come down
for that portal in the skin
Don't pierce your bodies with knives and
needles to let the demons in

# WHEN EVIL WAS ENEMY

When The Turks then struck and wounded The Bear
In the fog of war when it was unclear
When evil showed its sleight of hand
Make nations split when they should band

When The Turks then struck and wounded The Bear
In a tug of war when that would be fair
When evil throve upon the land
As nations split when they should band

# WHEN LOVE CAME KNOCKING

She was about sixteen, we can't be sure
When Love Came Knocking on her heart's door
Her butterfly kisses just flew away
With the sixteen years of her child's play
Another heart opened up and for good
When Love Came Knocking as it would
She sang love songs, word for word
Danced to a music that only she heard
It made life more difficult than years gone by
When Love Came Knocking and who knows why
And all the changes, they came so soon
From shaggy-haired dolls to Mills and Boon
But it changed her life and brought sweet dreams
When Love Came Knocking and so it seems

# WHEN PASSION CRIES

When passion cries
A heavy heart, a moment hard to bear
When passion cries
A silent tongue can't find the words to share
When passion cries
A feeling good and welled up tears of joy
When passion cries
A jilted girl goes crazy over boy
When passion cries
A thousand teardrops when a loved one dies
When passion cries
A very first time when that baby cries

# WHITHER, BLIND LADY

A sightless visionary as good as can be
Inspires the sighted and get them to see
She visits the sick and buries the dead
Tutors the young, be there when they wed
And walking a dog though thrice per week
One of her few little pleasures to seek
Long, long ago before she was blind
Such were the things, far from her mind
Leading by example day after day
Whither, Blind Lady, show us the way

# WINDOWS OF LIFE

Those screens we watch
are Windows of Life; in all
its glory, in all its strife; its
little joys, its big sorrows,
its fuzzy past and bright
tomorrows.

# WINTER'S TAIL

How stubborn, this tail of winter, you
can feel it in its sting
It's not over till it's over, when will the
fat lady sing

How reluctant this tail of winter, how
slowly it would swing
And how long it's taking Winter's Tail
to sweep us onto spring

# WOMEN

Growing stronger as
centuries turn
Rock the cradles, little
hands

Broke the glass-ceiling
so to learn
And to form all-female
bands

Would rather love but
not its spurn
Soon to end, those one
night stands

Dethroning kings as
kingdoms burn
Rule the roost and share
the lands

The DISTAFF SIDE,
is soon to yearn
Equidistant archers'
wands

# YOUR LIVES MATTER TOO

Your hopes and dreams are worth the fight
There is no doubt your cause is right
So when you rise up as you should
It had better be for good
Skeptics looking to deride
When fakers latch on to your side
But stay the course your goal is clear
Be it far or be it near

Printed in the United States
By Bookmasters